AMAZING GOD

by
JOHN UTLEY

To Mary
May our Amazing
God show Himself
real to you in 2020

P.O. Box 840
Granger, IN 46530

Photo of John Utley, courtesy of Dania Cueto (On Cue Photography)
Edited by Joanna Fredere
Cover design by Jonathan Utley, photo & border design
(ID:295382927 GaudiLab/Shutterstock.com) used under license from
shutterstock.com.

DEDICATION

To Susan, the most incredible wife, mother and friend.
Thanks for taking this journey with me!

CONTENTS

ACKNOWLEDGMENTS

This book would not be possible without many hands, hearts and eyes pouring over the details, making sure the participles are not dangling, and nouns find their subject.

First, I want to say thank you to my wife, Susan. She always believes in my dreams and rarely rolls her eyes when she hears another one. Thank you sweetheart for believing and taking the journey with me.

Second, special thanks to Joanna Fredere, arguably the best daughter ever. She put endless hours in scouring this book for every editable notion, dared to comma-tize the work with aplomb and when sleep screamed her name, she fought back with call outs and triple dots. She tamed the verb tenses like a lion tamer keeps the beast at bay. Thank you Joanna. You rock! And you shall be richly rewarded.

Third, thanks to Jonathan Utley for his cover design. Jonathan's eye for the subtle tweak makes me proud, although I still don't know how you did it. You are cool beyond cool. Thank you!

Fourth, thanks to Joshua Utley for his encouragement to keep on going. He cheers me on like a super hero. A little bit of Batman…but no capes, and no cheer leader outfits…thank God, but plenty of encouragement. Thanks Joshua!

Finally, thanks to the great people at Radiant Life. The leadership team, staff and the entire church make my life a Radiant Life and make the calling of God totally awesome.

INTRODUCTION

Have you ever considered the word, "AMAZING?" Its definition means "causing great wonder; astonishing." The synonyms of amazing include astonishing, astounding, surprising, stunning, shocking, startling, and breathtaking.

A big word reserved for the wonder that something, or someone brings. The longer I live, the profound realization that He is an amazing God has grown. Through every trial and blessing, I have come to the belief that one of the best days of my life was the day I realized that God has always had my best interest at heart. He is an Amazing God. So, in light of that revelation, I felt the stirring to write this book.

Actually, a lot of inspiration came from people facing insurmountable odds. People who found God more amazing after the trial started than they knew when life was quiet.

In the pages that follow, I will attempt the impossible. I will try to reveal to the reader of this book the power, might, glory, and awesomeness of an AMAZING GOD! I will probably fail.

I will aspire to express God's interaction with saints of old, and connect them with His actions in your life.

I will try to expose the character of an Amazing God that may help you know Him better, with a deeper understanding, and with greater intimacy than ever before.

I seek to reveal God in a way that befits His amazing nature.

This fear of failure is probably a deep intrinsic fear that the extent of our amazing God is an impossibility to express in words. It is not within my vocabulary to find those depths, nor within my knowledge, nor within the relationship I have with God to fully express how amazing God is, for the journey He has me on is still revealing His nature.

So with this fear of failure, why try? Why attempt such an impossible task? Because people need to know the overwhelming truth that God is AMAZING. His actions, His love, His character, His holiness, His desires, His judgment, His love, and His anger all point to the one powerful fact that all that He is, and everything that He does, is amazing. He is an Amazing God!

If the actions of God portrayed in these next few pages reveal God's heart, if they cause a weary warrior to keep fighting, the bound captive to find freedom, the one lost in loneliness to find a friend that will walk side by side, the hurting to find a healer, the frustrated to find peace, I will be satisfied. I believe that for those who see Him as He desires to be seen, will have a profound understanding that God is Amazing.

The chapters that follow will take you on a journey with Moses and the Jews as they begin the process of discovering the Amazing God that their ancestor, Abraham knew. You will gaze upon God's interaction with them as He begins the process of revealing who He was to a people that only had an understanding of Him through the perspective of their captors.

They did not know God in any kind of personal way, and at best, it was a knowledge handed down from their parents and grandparents. It was an institutional understanding, one that was head knowledge but no heart association. They did not have a relationship with the God that desired to reveal Himself.

In the heart of God, there was a desire to be more than a religious figure in the lives of His people. He wanted them to know Him in an intimate way. He was amazing in all that He did, in who He was, and the Jews had no basis for understanding that truth.

The heart of God was for that to change. He wanted people to know Him, and in that process, He would do amazing things for them, not to create a sense of astonishment, but for people to see the wonder and breathtaking God for who He was...and is, and for that to translate in a deep, intimate, and awesome relationship. For the very first time in history, God would not reveal Himself just to an individual (Adam, Eve, Abraham, Noah, etc.), but to a nation.

He wanted to start with a man, Moses, reveal Himself to a people, the Jews, and then, in most epic fashion, reveal Himself to the individual so that a relationship could be established with each person.

He wanted to reveal Himself to everyone. Every.Single.One. Even you. Even me.

It started with the leader, Moses.

So with that in mind, let me share with you what I have discovered about this Amazing God!

CHAPTER 1

———◆◆———

I AM

It could almost sound like a 'once upon a time' kind of story, except this has no damsel in distress or princess in waiting. The reality of it, however, was designed for one purpose: to reveal an Amazing God.

It does begin with the "once upon a time, in a land far, far away" kind of way, though. A land harboring a fugitive named Moses. By the time this story finds him, he is settled into a pretty normal mundane life, very unlike a past which included being a man on the run. Now, he was a sheepherder a thousand miles away from civilization, at least the kind of civilization he knew growing up.

His life started in Egypt. A ruthless pharaoh, fearful that the Jews in his land would take over, ordered that every baby boy be thrown into the Nile River. Moses' mother hid her pregnancy, and after delivering a baby boy, she hid him for three months before finally deciding to put her baby boy in God's hands. She placed him in a basket and pushed him into the bulrushes…floating him toward his destiny. Pharaoh's wife found him, felt compassion, and called for a Jewish woman to nurse this child. In epic fashion, Moses' mother was the one chosen and paid to nurse her very own son.

No doubt that while she nursed her son, she shared the story of his people, his unbelievable rescue, and his Amazing God. Eventually though, she had to surrender her son to his destiny and the Jew named Moses was raised in the home of the king.

The fate of the rest of the Jews was not as kind. The Egyptians hated the Jews and treated them with extreme brutality.

Moses grew up with everything a boy could want…but He also grew up with an affinity for the Jewish people. One day, while visiting the Jewish people, he witnessed an Egyptian beating a Jewish slave. Moses was incensed with the brutality and killed the Egyptian. In a panic, he buried the body and then ran for his life…into a desolate desert far, far away.

Sometimes desert places turn into
defining moments…
and sometimes such defining moments
lead to incredible destinies.

Moses was a son of a king, but a fugitive from the law who was quietly living a mundane life as a shepherd.

One day Moses took his sheep to the edge of nowhere when a bush near him began to burn. It was not as curious to see a burning bush in the desert as it was to see one burn without being consumed by the flames…so Moses got closer to view this anomaly.

That was when fire and destiny met. A bush burning became a call to a journey.

At that burning bush, God spoke to Moses.

From that moment, the call of God was clear. It was not just a call to lead the people of Israel from Egypt to the Promised Land; it was an invitation to take a journey with

God. A journey that would reveal more than anyone had ever known about God.

That is your call today. God has not just called you to go from here to heaven, but to take a journey with Him. On this journey, He desires to reveal more about Himself to you than you have ever known. I am convinced that if you will view your journey the right way, you will see how Amazing God really is. Not in an "I can pull a rabbit out of an empty hat" kind of amazing - if that is your view of God, you have no doubt had great disappointment with God, which has led to a disillusioned perspective of His character.

That disillusionment will be profound, for you are not ever going to experience an Amazing God if you seek a magic trick, an illusion, or a manipulated mess masquerading as god.

It's time to get a new revelation of God! It's time to take an epic journey with an Amazing God.

That is just what Moses was about to do when we find him in his story.

He looked at the burning bush and God told Moses to take his sandals off, for the ground was holy. God revealed Himself as the God of the forefathers. Moses knew that He was in the midst of the very presence of God Himself and covered His face, fearing to look at God.

God called Moses to lead the people of Israel out of Egypt to a land that God had long-declared would belong to His people.

So, the first question Moses asked God was about himself: [11] But Moses protested to God, "Who am I to appear before Pharaoh? Who am I to lead the people of Israel out of Egypt?" (Exodus 3:11, NLT) If Moses was into titles, his certainly did not include "LEADER."

In his message series, "Crash the Chatterbox," based on his best-selling book by the same name, Steven Furtick[1] calls this moment the moment of insecurity in Moses' life. That moment of insecurity acts like a voice that calls out three areas of insecurity. As Steven shared, the first voice of insecurity laments: "I am so dysfunctional!"

Moses' first response to the Lord's command was not to question God's authority, but to highlight his own dysfunction. Even though the Lord spoke clearly and directly to him, Moses was quick to ask, "Who am I to do this?" This insecurity may have stemmed from the lingering guilt Moses had after killing an Egyptian.

Though some people have more visible dysfunctions than others, we all have some form of insecurity rooted in what seems to be an insurmountable dysfunction. You may echo that perception that somehow your dysfunction is too much to overcome to be used by God. However, there is no dysfunction so great in us that God cannot overcome it and do something through us.

---

[1] http://elevationchurch.org/sermons/i-know-i-am/

It may not be dysfunction that is strongest, but there may be this feeling that Moses echoed in the second insecurity: I AM SO DEFICIENT!

God gave Moses three powerful signs in Exodus 4 to prove His ability, but Moses was still hesitant to pursue the calling God placed on his life. Specifically, Moses questioned his ability to speak on the Lord's behalf. While Moses carried on his conversation with God, the voices in his head were hard at work within Moses' mind pointing out his deficiencies.

Moses, like we sometimes do, found himself reminding God of his inadequacies in order to convince Him to use someone else. Sometimes, like Moses, we feel that being known leaves us susceptible to failure and embarrassment. However, God made us, fully knows all our abilities and deficiencies, and still calls us to do the impossible.

When God exposes one of your insecurities, you are not doomed, but given an opportunity show the perfect strength of God. Your weakness in God's hands becomes strength. God can literally turn your greatest insecurity into a weapon that He can use mightily for His glory, one that will defeat your enemy.

If the tactic of pointing out your deficiency does not work, your enemy then begins to taunt your faith with the third insecurity Moses experienced: I AM SO DOUBTFUL! Even though God assured Moses that He would give Moses the words, Moses still asked God to send someone else. We don't always doubt God; we mostly doubt ourselves.

Steven Furtick said: "When we second-guess our ability, we're ultimately questioning God's craftsmanship... We're implying that He left something out whenever He put us together."

It is almost like there is a voice inside of us screaming, "I AM NEVER _____ ENOUGH," "I AM SO DYSFUNCTIONAL," "I AM SO DEFICIENT," "I AM SO DOUBTFUL" and then with perverted self-assurance we say, "I know I am."

Moses said, "Who am I to lead the people of Israel out of Egypt?" We say, "who am I to share the gospel," or "how can I do _____ for God, I am a nobody, "I know I am."

Many times, we too feel like we have messed up too much, bring too little to the table, or don't have enough of 'whatever' to be used of God. We tend to hide behind our need, our lack, our sin, and walk in the feeling that we are never good enough to do God's will.

We hide behind our title, or lack thereof, as being unqualified to obey God.

You can never overlook the possibility that God's desire is not just to get you from here to heaven. If he wanted to do that, he could have transported you on chariots of fire, with angels as your escort, directly to heaven when you repented and started your journey with Christ.

If it were only about getting you to heaven, God would take you now.

No, His intent is greater than that. He wants you to come to know this Amazing God in ways you have never known before. Your every battle, your every bit of bad news, your every situation along this route to the Promised Land is an opportunity for God to reveal Himself to you in greater ways.

You really don't know Him in the way He longs to be known.

You only know Him as much as your captors have told you.

You know as much as you have been told by those who don't know God as much as you need to know God.

God's desire is for you to see Him as Amazing as He has always been, and will always be!

God followed Moses' question with a powerful simple truth: "I will be with you..." (Exodus 3:12, NLT) Moses' mind must have been reeling. If he went to the people to tell them that God had spoken to them, how would they respond?

[13] But Moses protested, "If I go to the people of Israel and tell them, 'The God of your ancestors has sent me to you,' they will ask me, 'What is his name?' Then what should I tell them?" (Exodus 3:13, NLT)

Moses asked a very interesting question: *"if they ask me 'What is his name?' Then what should I tell them?"* That was a strange question because the people already knew His name.

The Expositor's Bible Commentary says this about verse 13:

"Moses did not anticipate being asked, "By what name is this deity called?" by Jews in Egypt. Rather, he feared that if he announced that the God of their fathers, the patriarchs, had sent him to them, they would bluntly ask him, "What is his name?" The point of their question was not the same as "Who is this God?" That question would have been answered: "He is called Yahweh." ...What they needed to know was "What does that name mean or signify in circumstances such as we are in?"[2]

They already knew Him as Yahweh...but what good would that do the people? They already knew His name.

When Moses delivered the message from God, the children of Israel would certainly want to know what His name meant for them.

They wanted to know the significance of it - His character; the quality of their God - and what that name should mean to them on the day Moses declared God's intent.

Moses was going to a people who had become slaves. The Jews, God's chosen people, were making bricks in the middle of nowhere, probably feeling like they were banished...forgotten even...by a God who in times past, revealed Himself in amazing ways!

They, who were the favored, were now forgotten.

You have probably felt the same. You are the favored of the Lord...the redeemed...a child of the King...one who belongs to God. Then, out of nowhere, something happens. Your world is turned upside down and you find yourself wondering, "Where is God? I thought I knew Him...I thought He knew me."

For the Jews, life in Egypt started well. They were favored

---

[2] Kaiser, W. C., Jr. (1990). Exodus. In F. E. Gaebelein (Ed.), *The Expositor's Bible Commentary: Genesis, Exodus, Leviticus, Numbers* (Vol. 2, p. 320). Grand Rapids, MI: Zondervan Publishing House.

by the leaders because of Joseph's dream interpretation. The nation of Egypt was saved because of him and God, and while he lived, the Jewish people were loved and appreciated for Joseph's sake. Unfortunately, a new leader emerged who did not know the story of Joseph, and jealousy and discontent set in. The favored became slaves.

That is why Moses wanted to know how to deal with a disappointed people, who would want to know what a message from God meant to them personally.

They would not want a just a name, they already had that; they needed a fresh revelation of God. They would want more than a cliché, they wanted something real.

They would want to know what it all meant…they would want to know what God's intent was…and what they could hold on to that would outlast their suffering.

The same is true for us. We may start well, blessed and favored. But over time, the enemy steals, kills, and destroys and it seems like God has abandoned us.

We reach a point when every cliché falls flat. When the cute sayings and memes run dry. When we long for something real, lasting and strong.

Most give up when the cliché's are not enough. Or they have a false epiphany from the devil that is a sudden and profound understanding, but it's framed the wrong way.

We have all seen those who have had that moment, where slaves who were bound by their circumstances hear the devil say that God has abandoned them. In that one sudden moment, they believe it, and it frames everything else in their lives.

They have a jaded outlook on life and God. It is a false epiphany from the devil that God wants to destroy with a fresh revelation of an Amazing God.

The question that Moses posed to God had profound implications. The people would not settle for anything other than a powerful revelation of God reaching into their circumstances. They were jaded and their circumstances needed more than a name...they needed a present God to deliver them.

So, God hears the question, what do I tell the people your name is? God answers: [14] God replied to Moses, "I AM WHO I AM. Say this to the people of Israel: I AM has sent me to you." (Exodus 3:14, NLT) What did God tell Moses? Tell them I AM has sent me to you.

I AM. This one verse has been debated for thousands of years. It was not an evasion of the question. It was not a reluctance to disclose His name, or His nature. It was not an attempt to cut Moses short. It was a connecting of His name "YAHWEH" and the ever present reality of God in their lives.

I AM.

He did not say, "I WAS."

In that moment, He did not connect with the past. He did not say, "I was the God of Abraham, Isaac, and Jacob." Nor did He declare, "I was the one that told Abraham that his seed would be more innumerable than the sands on the seashore." He did not make a point of His work by looking back at the time that he provided a wife for Isaac, not the time He revealed a ladder with angels ascending and descending before Jacob. He did not reveal Himself as the one who wrestled with Jacob. He did not say, "I WAS."

He did not say, "I MIGHT."

If I am in the mood…if I am feeling just so-so…if you push the right buttons…if you do enough good things…if you meet the criteria. I might help you…He did not say, "I MIGHT."

He did not say, "I WILL."

I will do something in the future…I will be out there when you need me…I will promise you that at some point I will do whatever you need. He did not say, "I WILL."

He did not say, "I DID."

He did not say I did great things when I delivered Joseph, I did great things when Lot needed to escape…He did not say, "I DID."

He did not say, "I SHOULD"

I should deliver the people. He did not say, "Moses, you know I was getting around to doing something…I should have, could have…would have….He did not say, "I SHOULD."

He did not say, "I CAN."

He did not say "I can do that…I can do all things…I can make it happen…I can be that God you need." Although He can do anything, they did not need to see a forward looking God, they needed a present help in times of trouble. He did not say, "I CAN."

He said, "I AM."

I Am God. I Am present. I Am able. I Am here. I Am now. I Am all you need.

I AM…

It was a revelation of the highest order. It was a rendering of all that the people needed, wanted, longed for, and hungered after…all rolled into one.

I AM.

Even before He made the declaration of His power, he told Moses his intent:

⁷ Then the LORD told him, "I have certainly seen the oppression of my people in Egypt. I have heard their cries of distress because of their harsh slave drivers. Yes, I am aware of their suffering. ⁸ So I have come down to rescue them from the power of the Egyptians and lead them out of Egypt into their own fertile and spacious land. It is a land flowing with milk and honey—the land where the Canaanites, Hittites, Amorites, Perizzites, Hivites, and Jebusites now live. ⁹ Look! The cry of the people of Israel has reached me, and I have seen how harshly the Egyptians abuse them. ¹⁰ Now go, for I am sending you to Pharaoh. You must lead my people Israel out of Egypt." (Exodus 3:7-10, NLT)

God was about to send the Jewish people on an incredible journey from Egypt to the Promised Land. This journey would be filled with opposition and opportunities…they would experience fear and favor…weariness and rest.

They did not need to know God would be where they were going; they needed God to be there every step of the way.

That's why he said, "I AM".

When you face trouble, I am powerful.

When you face fear, I am here.

When the enemy comes in like a flood, I am greater.

I AM.

[15] God also said to Moses, "Say this to the people of Israel: Yahweh, the God of your ancestors—the God of Abraham, the God of Isaac, and the God of Jacob—has sent me to you. This is my eternal name, my name to remember for all generations. (Exodus 3:15, NLT)

God told Moses to tell the children of Israel, "I AM has sent me to you."

"I AM" is an amazing phrase also used by Jesus in the New Testament.

In John 6:35, [35] Jesus replied, "I am the bread of life. Whoever comes to me will never be hungry again. Whoever believes in me will never be thirsty. (NLT)

John 8:12 records another "I am" statement when the Bible records that: [12] Jesus spoke to the people once more and said, "I am the light of the world. If you follow me, you won't have to walk in darkness, because you will have the light that leads to life." (NLT)

Another "I am" statement is found in John 10:9 "[9] Yes, I am the gate. Those who come in through me will be saved. They will come and go freely and will find good pastures." (NLT)

His "I am" intent is found again in John 10:11 "[11] "I am the good shepherd. The good shepherd sacrifices his life for the sheep."(NLT)

Again, he declares, "I am" when talking about death in John 11:25: ²⁵ Jesus told her, "I am the resurrection and the life. Anyone who believes in me will live, even after dying. ²⁶ Everyone who lives in me and believes in me will never ever die. (NLT)

John 14:6 is another "I am" statement, but this one reveals Jesus as the ONLY WAY to the Father: ⁶ Jesus told him, "I am the way, the truth, and the life. No one can come to the Father except through me. (NLT)

Jesus declared, "I AM" and his intent in John 15:1 "I am the true grapevine, and my Father is the gardener." (NLT) But it was the following statement that sent the Jews over the edge. They were arguing with Jesus over who He was...and this was the conversation:

⁵² The people said, "Now we know you are possessed by a demon. Even Abraham and the prophets died, but you say, 'Anyone who obeys my teaching will never die!' ⁵³ Are you greater than our father Abraham? He died, and so did the prophets. Who do you think you are?" ⁵⁴ Jesus answered, "If I want glory for myself, it doesn't count. But it is my Father who will glorify me. You say, 'He is our God,' ⁵⁵ but you don't even know him. I know him. If I said otherwise, I would be as great a liar as you! But I do know him and obey him. ⁵⁶ Your father Abraham rejoiced as he looked forward to my coming. He saw it and was glad." ⁵⁷ The people said, "You aren't even fifty years old. How can you say you have seen Abraham?" ⁵⁸ Jesus answered, "I tell you the truth, before Abraham was even born, I Am!" (John 8:52-58, NLT)

A Greek Scholar by the name of Ethelbert Stauffer states that "the phrase harbors within itself the most authentic, the most audacious, and the most profound affirmation by Jesus of who he was."[3]

Even when they came to arrest Jesus, on the night he was betrayed, and just hours before he was crucified, the Bible shares one last "I AM" statement from Jesus.

In John 18, the Bible describes the events this way: [3] The leading priests and Pharisees had given Judas a contingent of Roman soldiers and Temple guards to accompany him. Now with blazing torches, lanterns, and weapons, they arrived at the olive grove. [4] Jesus fully realized all that was going to happen to him, so he stepped forward to meet them. "Who are you looking for?" he asked. [5] "Jesus the Nazarene," they replied. "I AM he," Jesus said. (Judas, who betrayed him, was standing with them.) [6] As Jesus said "I AM he," they all drew back and fell to the ground! (NLT)

In the original Greek, verse five simply says, "I AM."

In each of these "I Am" statements in John represent a particular relationship of Jesus to meet your spiritual needs.

He then becomes your light in the darkness, your security and fellowship, your guide and protector, your hope in death, your certainty in perplexity, and your

[3] Tenney, M. C. (1981). John. In F. E. Gaebelein (Ed.), *The Expositor's Bible Commentary: John and Acts* (Vol. 9, p. 99). Grand Rapids, MI: Zondervan Publishing House.

source of life.

You probably have not had a burning bush experience, but you may have had a 'burning heart' moment, where you felt a gentle whisper in your spirit, or a tug of your heart towards God. Those moments are just as powerful as they declare to you that God has intents for you that are for 'good and not evil, to give you a future and a hope.'

God wants to reveal Himself to you in greater ways than you have ever known!

> *He wants you to know Him,*
> *not for what He can give you,*
> *but for who He can be to you!*

For Moses, everything that would happen would be predicated on this thought: "I am" is with me. "I am" is present. "I am" is here.

Every battle, every stopping place, every enemy, every dry and thirsty place, every place of hunger is another place for God to show up. Another place for God to make it happen. Another place to reveal His incredible nature. Another place of greater revelation of our Amazing God.

Unfortunately, I have not arrived at this place yet. I still get discouraged. I still wonder. I still come to hungry places and wonder why I don't have what I want to eat. I come to thirsty places and can't find anything to satisfy my thirst. I still feel dysfunctional, deficient and doubtful.

When I feel that "I am dysfunctional, I am deficient, I am

doubtful, and I know I am" then that understanding only intensifies my lack and inability. It gains its power to keep me from doing what God has destined for me to do simply because I am looking at me, and what I cannot do. But I know know God, I know the "I AM" that Moses knew, and because I know: "I AM"…then that relationship changes everything. I may still say, "I am dysfunctional, I am deficient, I am doubtful," because it is true, but the game changer is this: I am all of those things, but I know "I AM" and because I know Him, that makes all the difference in the world!

Because I know "I AM," then my journey can come alive with the presence and power of God.

In His presence there is fullness of joy.

In His presence, there is peace that passes understanding.

In His presence, I have water when I am thirsty.

In His presence, I have food when I am hungry.

He wants to reveal that to me every day.

Why do I complain when I have the great I AM with me? And because I KNOW HIM…I am going to be alright!

Our journey, just like that of Moses and the Jews, is designed to take us deeper into the knowledge that I AM is here and HE IS Amazing. Once you come into this understanding, you will see that He is, truly, an AMAZING GOD!

CHAPTER 2

The Table is Set

The battle is not just about you.

Your problems are not just about you. Your storms are not just focused on you and are not simply about your situation. If God allowed the trial, it is about more than just you. It is also about your enemy.

Let us define the word "enemy." Your enemy is not your boss, your ex, your teacher, your wayward teenager, or your spouse. Your enemy is not a physical entity. And, certainly, your enemy is not God.

Your true enemy is an unseen being, one whose sole aim is your eternal destruction. He is known as Lucifer, Satan, the devil, Beelzebub…etc. Regardless of the moniker, he wants to separate you from God for eternity. He will stand in the way, get in the way, distract you from the way, and frustrate you all along the way. He is at war with God and you are caught in the middle.

His goal is to make the sacrifice of Jesus on the cross of no consequence to you. You are the prize he longs to claim, and once taken, he will discard you like trash for eternity.

God, on the other hand, so loved you that He sent His son Jesus to the world to die for your sins. Jesus died so you could be free, so you could know God personally, and so He could spend eternity with you in the most beautiful, fantastic place ever imagined.

God is not against you but He IS against Satan.

God will use your problem to show Himself mighty and strong, but it's not just for you. He will use your problem to draw you closer to Himself. He will also use your problem against your enemy.

God wants to set a table before you
in the presence of your enemy.

This truth is what Moses would find to be profound. After Moses had the dramatic encounter with God at the burning bush, he traveled back to Egypt, met Aaron, talked to the children of Israel, and then went before Pharaoh.

Both Moses and Aaron told Pharaoh that the Lord had instructed them to go into the wilderness and worship the Lord...but Pharaoh says in Exodus 5:2, ""And who is the LORD? Why should I listen to him and let Israel go? I don't know the LORD, and I will not let Israel go." (Exodus 5:2, NLT)

Pharaoh was very clear. He had no knowledge of or respect for the Lord. Pharaoh accused Moses and Aaron of distracting the people. So, Pharaoh ordered the slave drivers to increase the load, making them get their own straw in their brick-making work. His goal was to burden them down so much that the Jews would turn on Moses.

Instead, it moved God to action against Pharaoh.

Exodus 7 reads:

¹ Then the LORD said to Moses, "Pay close attention to this.

I will make you seem like God to Pharaoh, and your brother, Aaron, will be your prophet. [2] Tell Aaron everything I command you, and Aaron must command Pharaoh to let the people of Israel leave his country. [3] But I will make Pharaoh's heart stubborn so I can multiply my miraculous signs and wonders in the land of Egypt. [4] Even then Pharaoh will refuse to listen to you. So I will bring down my fist on Egypt. Then I will rescue my forces—my people, the Israelites—from the land of Egypt with great acts of judgment. [5] When I raise my powerful hand and bring out the Israelites, the Egyptians will know that I am the LORD." (NLT)

For the Egyptian people, Pharaoh was a godlike being. He was revered by the people, "Of course, the king was also subject to some rather grave responsibilities. Through his dealings with the gods, he was tasked with keeping the order … therefore keeping out chaos, often in the form of the enemies of Egypt from foreign lands. But he was also responsible for making sufficient offerings and otherwise satisfying the gods so that they would bless Egypt with a bountiful Nile flood, and therefore a good enough harvest to feed his people. When he failed at these tasks, he could bear not only blame, but a weakening of the state and thus his power."[4]

So, now the fight was on, and the battle between the 'godlike' Pharaoh and the "you will seem like a God to

---

[4] http://www.touregypt.net/featurestories/pharaohs.htm#ixzz3mlTGGIsG

Pharaoh, Moses" began.

God would send ten plagues, arranged in groups of three.

The first of each three found the confrontation of God and Pharaoh as he is on his way to the Nile. This could have been a time when Pharaoh was on his way to worship the Nile river god. It was a direct confrontation with Pharaoh who was like a god and the god he was worshipping.

The second of each three was introduced as a warning, but these occurred at Pharaoh's palace. The place of power for Pharaoh and the nation of Egypt would stand in contrast to the shepherds-staff wielding Moses and Aaron.

The final of the three came without warning to Pharaoh. They were set in motion by Moses and Aaron with a clear understanding of the plague's origin.

One commentator noted that the first of the three groups were designed so that Pharaoh would know that THE GREAT I AM is the Lord. The second was so that Moses and the children of Israel would know that the LORD is GOD OVER EVERY THING. The third set was so that every one would know that there is NO ONE like the LORD. [5]

This same concept applies every time you face a trial. God wants your enemy to know that HE IS THE LORD. He wants you to know HE IS THE LORD.

He wants everyone to know NO ONE is like the Lord. He

---

[5] Kaiser, W. C., Jr. (1990). Exodus. In F. E. Gaebelein (Ed.), *The Expositor's Bible Commentary: Genesis, Exodus, Leviticus, Numbers* (Vol. 2, p. 348). Grand Rapids, MI: Zondervan Publishing House.

is truly AMAZING!

Your trial is not just about you. That revelation will change your trials if you see them for what they are…an opportunity for God to reveal HIMSELF to you in a greater way. They are an opportunity for God to show up your enemy, and your trials serve as a testimony to those around you. The ultimate goal of the plagues was not to punish as much as it was about divine revelation - for both Pharaoh and the Jews.

The first three plagues were irritations. The Jews suffered alongside the Egyptians. Sometimes people suffer because of their hard heartedness and God's people suffer too.

The first plague is found in Exodus 7:14. The Bible says that Pharaoh's heart was stubborn. Even though God knew Pharaoh's heart, that hard heart did not change Pharaoh's ability to choose. As the story begins, Pharaoh was going down to the river…a usual practice to worship the god of the Nile. Moses and Aaron interrupted his worship with a confrontation from God.

Aaron raised his staff and struck the water of the Nile. Suddenly the whole river turned to blood. The fish died, and the river became so foul the people could not drink it. There was blood throughout the land. This blood touched everything and were in all of the normal locations of water. The magicians of Egypt were able to replicate something that looked like the same thing. The only thing was they were replicating judgment from God. This was not helpful at all, but at least in their minds, they looked like they had power.

Anytime we try to take matters in our own hands, we end

with the same fate: A worsening situation, and like this story, the end result stinks.

The Bible says that Pharaoh returned to his palace and tried to put the whole thing out of his mind.

That is one of the greatest frustrations for God's people. When God does something so powerful and demonstrates that He is God, we sometimes feel that by this act alone, people will readily repent. When evil people see God's hand, and they will automatically turn to him in repentance.

That is seldom the case.

Why? People are spiritually blind. The Apostle Paul wrote about this phenomenon in 2 Corinthians 4 ...

"[3] If the Good News we preach is hidden behind a veil, it is hidden only from people who are perishing. [4] Satan, who is the god of this world, has blinded the minds of those who don't believe. They are unable to see the glorious light of the Good News. They don't understand this message about the glory of Christ, who is the exact likeness of God. (NLT)

The activity of God does not always translate into open hearts for people who are blinded to truth. We should pray for their eyes of understanding to be opened.

After the river turned to blood, Pharaoh refused to budge, so God told Moses and Aaron to tell Pharaoh a plague of frogs would invade the land. Frogs will jump, climb, and be in everything - beds, in ovens, in kneading bowls. They will jump on people; they will infect the land with amphibian chaos, and affect everything and everyone. Pharaoh refused to let the people go, so Aaron raised his staff and frogs were everywhere. EVERYWHERE!

Meals were chaos, with frogs jumping and creating noise. Naps for babies were meaningless, and even a simple walk down the sidewalk would have been a chore as frogs covered the land.

They were everywhere. They were in everything.

I think it is comical because frogs were considered sacred by the Egyptians. Can you imagine that the very thing you worship is driving you mad? The spiritual principle is very powerful:

Sometimes you get what you worship in abundance, so make sure you are worshipping the right God.

If someone is worshipping some *thing*, that very thing can invade their lives in abundance. If they worship money, it will invade their lives. Not an abundance of money, but an abundance of irritation. If they are chasing after the dollar, they will have loss in abundance...such as losing their family, losing sleep, losing peace, and perhaps even losing their soul as they search for more.

Like the frogs did in Egypt, what we worship will invade every part of our life...food, rest, sleep, everything. It will consume us. God will not have any god before Him and anyone chasing after anything but God will lack true satisfaction and peace. Frogs were everywhere, and Pharaoh asked Moses to get rid of them, promising he would let the people go in return.

In response, Moses did something strange. He asked Pharaoh when he wanted the frogs to leave. It seems to be a strange request, but Pharaoh's response is even stranger still: Pharaoh said, "get rid of them tomorrow morning." Most everyone would want to be rid of these pests immediately. Pharaoh, however, was content to live one more night with the source of his frustration.

All around us are people who want to be free from their bondage, but only on their terms. Alcoholics will get rid of the drink, but only on their terms. Drug addicts will quit, but only on their terms. Unfortunately, their desire for control will continue to affect their lives, through the night, and maybe through the rest of their lives. Surrender is the key, but for Pharaoh, and for many around us, surrender is not an option they consider plausible.

Moses prayed and the next day, the frogs all died. The Bible says the people created mounds of frog carcasses. A very unpleasant sight and smell, no doubt.

Without warning to Pharaoh, the next plague was introduced when Aaron struck the dust, and at that, the dust became gnats. The magicians of the land could not replicate this plague. They had seen enough to declare to Pharaoh: [19] "This is the finger of God!" the magicians exclaimed to Pharaoh. But Pharaoh's heart remained hard. He wouldn't listen to them, just as the LORD had predicted. (Exodus 8:19, NLT)

This was another irritation, and gnats covered people and animals alike. God was seeking to reveal himself to the children of Israel and the nation of Egypt. Up until now, there was no indication that these plagues had any effect on the children of Israel except irritation.

After this, God sends the second of the three sets of plagues.

The second three were destructions that did not touch the Jews.

Sometimes when evil causes an action, it affects believers, and sometimes it doesn't.

Early one morning as Pharaoh was again down to the Nile, possibly to worship his river god, Pharaoh was confronted by Moses and Aaron again. They told him,

'This is what the LORD says: Let my people go, so they can worship me. ²¹ If you refuse, then I will send swarms of flies on you, your officials, your people, and all the houses. The Egyptian homes will be filled with flies, and the ground will be covered with them. ²² But this time I will spare the region of Goshen, where my people live. No flies will be found there. Then you will know that I am the LORD and that I am present even in the heart of your land. ²³ I will make a clear distinction between my people and your people. This miraculous sign will happen tomorrow.' " (Exodus 8:20-23, NLT)

With this plague, the people had plenty of time to repent since the flies were to arrive the next day, but this time, there would be no flies where the Jews lived. For the first time in this time of confrontation, there is a distinction between the Jews and the Egyptians.

These flies were not the garden-variety houseflies that fly around your screen door, and you kill them because they are pestering you. These particular flies were biting flies. They were everywhere and biting everyone, except the Jews. Scripture relates that the whole land of Egypt was thrown into chaos because of the flies.

Because of the flies, Pharaoh agreed to let them offer sacrifices, but only in the land they were currently living...he still refused to let them go. Moses refused and Pharaoh finally said, "Alright, go and worship your God, but pray for me." So, Moses prayed and the flies left. But Pharaoh changed his mind and refused to let the people leave.

Because of Pharaoh's stubbornness, God told Moses and Aaron to tell Pharaoh that the next plague would affect livestock. And again, there would be a distinction between Egypt and the people of Israel. The Jews would not lose any animals to the plague.

Another part of Egypt's wide array of gods was hard hit: the Apis, or sacred bull Ptah; the calf god Ra; the cows of Hathor; the jackal-headed god Anubis; and the bull Bakis of the god Mentu. The evidence was too strong to be mere coincidence: the time was set by Yahweh, the God of the Hebrews (v.5); (2) a "distinction" was made between the cattle of the two peoples (v.4); and (3) the results were total: all Egyptian cattle "in the field" (v.3) died; not one head of Israelite livestock perished.[6]

---

[6] Kaiser, W. C., Jr. (1990). Exodus. In F. E. Gaebelein (Ed.), *The Expositor's Bible Commentary: Genesis, Exodus, Leviticus, Numbers* (Vol. 2,

The next one, which completes the second cycle, was sent unannounced. For the first time the lives of humans were attacked and endangered.

With a touch of divine irony and poetic justice, Moses and Aaron were each to take two handfuls of soot from the brick-making furnace, the symbol of Israel's bondage (v.8; see 1:14; 5:7–19). The soot was to be placed in a container and carried to Pharaoh's presence, where Moses then tossed it into the air. There was also a logical connection between the soot created by the sweat of God's enslaved people and the judgment that was to afflict the bodies of the enslavers. When the soot was tossed skyward, festering boils broke out on all the Egyptians and their animals (vv.9–10). [7]

Even the magicians could not stand in the presence of Pharaoh due to the pain the boils brought to them.

It is imperative to see that God could have rescued Israel; in His mighty power he could have destroyed the people of Egypt before any plague came. He could have sent destruction and killed everyone and not dealt with Pharaoh, or the Egyptians at all. However, God's goal is for all to know Him. Everyone, including the enemy.

It seems that the intensity of the plagues increased with each

pp. 357–358). Grand Rapids, MI: Zondervan Publishing House.

[7] Kaiser, W. C., Jr. (1990). Exodus. In F. E. Gaebelein (Ed.), *The Expositor's Bible Commentary: Genesis, Exodus, Leviticus, Numbers* (Vol. 2, pp. 357–358). Grand Rapids, MI: Zondervan Publishing House.

succeeding plague.

The seventh plague finds Pharaoh on his way to the Nile River to offer sacrifices to the river god again, which by now probably seemed futile because his god was not helping at all. So Exodus 9 reads:

¹³ Then the LORD said to Moses, "Get up early in the morning and stand before Pharaoh. Tell him, 'This is what the LORD, the God of the Hebrews, says: Let my people go, so they can worship me. ¹⁴ If you don't, I will send more plagues on you and your officials and your people. Then you will know that there is no one like me in all the earth. ¹⁵ By now I could have lifted my hand and struck you and your people with a plague to wipe you off the face of the earth. ¹⁶ But I have spared you for a purpose—to show you my power and to spread my fame throughout the earth. ¹⁷ But you still lord it over my people and refuse to let them go. ¹⁸ So tomorrow at this time I will send a hailstorm more devastating than any in all the history of Egypt. ¹⁹ Quick! Order your livestock and servants to come in from the fields to find shelter. Any person or animal left outside will die when the hail falls.' " ²⁰ Some of Pharaoh's officials were afraid because of what the LORD had said. They quickly brought their servants and livestock in from the fields. ²¹ But those who paid no attention to the word of the LORD left theirs out in the open. (NLT)

Even though this was going to be the most severe plague so far, it was grace that God informed them at all about this plague. God warned them in time for them to get their families inside and their livestock out of the fields (what livestock were left). It was the grace of God displayed for all to see.

Sometimes we wonder why God doesn't strike evildoers down right where they walk. It is His grace that is in play.

That is true today! We sometimes wonder why God delays His justice, but Peter shares the heart of God in 2 Peter 3:9:

⁹ The Lord isn't really being slow about his promise, as some people think. No, he is being patient for your sake. He does not want anyone to be destroyed, but wants everyone to repent. (NLT)

The heart for everyone to repent has been around for a long time, and I believe that Pharaoh could have repented, but continued to refuse God.

Moses lifted has staff to the sky, hail rained down…and everything outside was gone. Except where the Jews lived. They were alive, well, and the kids were probably playing outside without any harm.

It sounds like Pharaoh has a change of heart:

²⁷ Then Pharaoh quickly summoned Moses and Aaron. "This time I have sinned," he confessed. "The LORD is the righteous one, and my people and I are wrong. ²⁸ Please beg the LORD to end this terrifying thunder and hail. We've had enough. I will let you go; you don't need to stay any longer." ²⁹ "All right," Moses replied. "As soon as I leave the city, I will lift my hands and pray to the LORD. Then the thunder and hail will stop, and you will know that the earth belongs to the LORD. ³⁰ But I know that you and your officials still do not fear the LORD God." (Exodus 9:27-30, NLT)

Moses did and the hail stopped, but unfortunately,

Pharaoh's heart was hard and he refused to let the people go.

That is the scariest thing for everyone hearing the voice of God. In His gentle way, God will lead us, guide us, and speak to us. Every time we obey His voice, or His prompting, we set ourselves up for blessing and favor. When we refuse, oppose, turn away, ignore, or otherwise disregard God's voice, we set our heart up for a hardening action.

Even though Pharaoh's heart hardened, his ability to choose was never taken from him. The natural process of pushing back against God's work in our lives results in hardened hearts.

Pharaoh could have repented at any time and it sounds like he did but he only wanted relief, not repentance. Exodus 9:35 says,

35 Because his heart was hard, Pharaoh refused to let the people leave, just as the LORD had predicted through Moses. (NLT)

The eighth plague finds Moses and Aaron confronting Pharaoh in his palace:

Then the LORD said to Moses, "Return to Pharaoh and make your demands again. I have made him and his officials stubborn so I can display my miraculous signs among them. 2 I've also done it so you can tell your children and grandchildren about how I made a mockery of the Egyptians and about the signs I displayed among them—and so you will know that I am the LORD." (Exodus 10:1-2, NLT)

This plague was as much about showing Israel who He was, as it was about showing Egypt that He alone was the LORD.

Some wonder in these stories why God did not just let them believe the way they believed. "Live and let live!"

In reality, that is the most dangerous practice. Every person has a soul, destined to spend eternity somewhere. For those who have accepted God's gift of salvation, that eternal place is beyond comparison. A place of peace, joy, and eternal life. A beauty that surpasses any location on planet earth.

Moreover, it is a place where death no longer is experienced, sickness is finished, evil is banished, and everyone is in the presence of God Himself. The incomparable joy there has never been experienced here.

For those who reject God's gift, the opposite is true. That place will be filled with darkness, weeping, pain, and misery such as never known here. A hell worse than any hell experienced on earth and the worse part is that those who refuse will be banished from God's presence for eternity.

I believe that is the "hell" of hell.

God wants people to know Him because all other gods are not gods at all. Simply man-made constructs that are not benign at all, but very dangerous to the eternal destination of every person.

Even though Pharaoh refused, God is always about declaring the truth of who He is. God told Moses to tell Pharaoh that a plague of locusts would invade the land and they would eat all of what was left after the hail had destroyed the crops. The leaders in Egypt begged Pharaoh to let he people go as they could not take another plague, but Pharaoh refused to let them go.

Then, as Moses warned, an army of locusts swarmed the land. Their ruthless attack on the land touched all the crops of the Egyptians, but the Jews were not affected at all.

The ninth plague came without warning to Pharaoh or the people of Egypt; this plague was extreme darkness. This darkness was so profound that the darkness could be felt, like a creepy, damp, and cold basement without light. A thick darkness intensified by evil.

Not so in Goshen, where the Jews lived, for there, it was a bright, sun-shining day.

The Egyptian god, "Ra," the god Egyptians credited with creation was worshipped as the sun god, but on this day, their god was nothing compared to the GREAT I AM. Virtually every god the Egyptians had worshipped, every god they had trusted in, every god they believed was true and real was now made to be nothing compared with the ONE TRUE GOD.

For such a people, once such kingdoms have been cast down, there is not a shred of a god worth worshipping.

God did not do this prove to the other 'gods' that He was the best god. All the other gods were not gods at all, and they certainly did not pose any threat to God. Their threat was to the people whose soul was eternal and whose worship endangered their very souls.

God wanted to set a table before the Jews in the presence of their enemies. In that presence, all other 'gods' surrender completely.

God will use our trials to reveal the 'gods' we have come to trust in, or rely on, that are not gods at all. But even if we have not bowed down before other gods, and serve Him faithfully, we can rest assured that He will set a table before us in the presence of our enemies to reveal Himself more fully, and in the process, we will find out how amazing God really is.

Unlike these false gods, He never fails, and His grace, love, and power set us up for greater revelation of who He is…and with these nine plagues, God desired to show the Jews, and their enemies, that He is truly an Amazing God.

The final plague took that premise to an even greater height.

CHAPTER 3

DELIVERER!

It's a new day. An opportunity for an Amazing God to reveal more about Himself. For the final plague, however, it was not just a revelation to the Egyptians, nor was it a revelation only to the Jews. It would change everything, for everyone, including you and me. This was THE plague that introduced a template for an eternal covenant.

Exodus 11 opens up with an eternal template:

Then the LORD said to Moses, "I will strike Pharaoh and the land of Egypt with one more blow. After that, Pharaoh will let you leave this country. In fact, he will be so eager to get rid of you that he will force you all to leave. ² Tell all the Israelite men and women to ask their Egyptian neighbors for articles of silver and gold." ³ (Now the LORD had caused the Egyptians to look favorably on the people of Israel. And Moses was considered a very great man in the land of Egypt, respected by Pharaoh's officials and the Egyptian people alike.) ⁴ Moses had announced to Pharaoh, "This is what the LORD says: At midnight tonight I will pass through the heart of Egypt. ⁵ All the firstborn sons will die in every family in Egypt, from the oldest son of Pharaoh, who sits on his throne, to the oldest son of his lowliest servant girl who grinds the flour. Even the firstborn of all the livestock will die. ⁶ Then a loud wail will rise throughout the land of Egypt, a wail like no one has heard before or will ever hear again. ⁷ But among the Israelites it will be so peaceful that not even a dog will bark. Then you will know that the LORD makes a distinction between the Egyptians and the Israelites. ⁸ All the officials of Egypt will run to me and fall to the ground before me. 'Please leave!' they will beg. 'Hurry! And take all your followers with you.' Only then will I go!" Then, burning with anger, Moses left Pharaoh. (Exodus 11:1-10, NLT)

There is no mention that Moses described any remedy for the final plague to Pharaoh. He only told him the effects of the plague. There <u>was</u> a remedy but only for those who were obedient to it's requirements. They alone found the answer to the plague that would bring about death to many.

God could have warned Pharaoh of the impending disaster and given him the remedy to help the people. It would not have helped, however because Pharaoh and the Egyptians were spiritually blind. There was no move toward repentance in any of the previous plagues and their responses were for the effects to end, not for a relationship with the God of the Jews.

The purpose of the plague was to reveal a God who wanted a relationship with mankind and not just a remedy to keep people safe.

Sometimes in a misguided attempt to see people saved, the gospel is dumbed down to a quick prayer without a call to life change. It then becomes a remedy, but without repentance, it ends there.

Some cut that short. Some want the remedy without the relationship. They want to pray a prayer and keep living like they never prayed the prayer.

God wants to do more than provide a remedy, He wants a relationship with men and women, boys and girls, and any attempt to seek a remedy without it will always fall short.

I believe that is why John the Baptist called out the Pharisees and Sadducees that came to watch him baptize individuals in Matthew 3:

7 But when he saw many Pharisees and Sadducees coming to watch him baptize, he denounced them. "You brood of snakes!" he exclaimed. "Who warned you to flee God's coming wrath? 8 Prove by the way you live that you have repented of your sins and turned to God. 9 Don't just say to each other, 'We're safe, for we are descendants of Abraham.' That means nothing, for I tell you, God can create children of Abraham from these very stones. 10 Even now the ax of God's judgment is poised, ready to sever the roots of the trees. Yes, every tree that does not produce good fruit will be chopped down and thrown into the fire. (NLT)

It's not about a remedy. It's all about relationship! God is not just wanting to 'save you from judgment,' he wants a relationship with you. He certainly doesn't want people in heaven that despise him, but those that love Him, those that obey Him, those that make it their pursuit to pursue Him.

The final plague's outcome would be the death of the first born in every home. This plague would affect all the first born in each family unless they followed the requirements that God set up for the people. If they followed them, then the first born in that home would live…the angel of death would pass over the home.

It was not just a "get out of Egypt" free card that God was giving them, it was literally a template for the people to see and experience an event that would directly point the people to a redeemer…to a sacrifice that would do better than free them from a captor named Pharaoh or called Egypt, but would free them from their sin.

That would free us from our sin.

God would use this template to bring forth His ONE AND ONLY son into the world and by HIS death, bring us freedom from our bondage and set us free from the power of death.

Of all the plagues, this one spoke loudest of God's Amazing redeeming love, one that gazed down through the ages and set a paradigm for our salvation.

The instructions that were given to the children of Israel were very clear and specific.

Exodus 12 reads:

"While the Israelites were still in the land of Egypt, the LORD gave the following instructions to Moses and Aaron: ² "From now on, this month will be the first month of the year for you."

The final plague would be celebrated with the beginning of a new year; a new year with a frame of reference based on freedom. Every generation from now on would look at each beginning of the new year thinking back to the moment God set the Jews free from Egyptian bondage.

"³ Announce to the whole community of Israel that on the tenth day of this month each family must choose a lamb or a young goat for a sacrifice, one animal for each household. ⁴ If a family is too small to eat a whole animal, let them share with another family in the neighborhood. Divide the animal according to the size of each family and how much they can eat."

This was the day used to select a lamb for sacrifice for Passover. This day would become the same day that the people of Israel would use to select the lamb for sacrifice for every Passover they would celebrate thereafter. Every year for hundreds and thousands of years, this day would be the same.

This is the same day when the Bible records that Jesus came into Jerusalem, riding on a donkey. It was called the Triumphant Entry and the story can be found in Matthew 21:

As Jesus and the disciples approached Jerusalem, they came to the town of Bethphage on the Mount of Olives. Jesus sent two of them on ahead. ² "Go into the village over there," he said. "As soon as you enter it, you will see a donkey tied there, with its colt beside it. Untie them and bring them to me. ³ If anyone asks what you are doing, just say, 'The Lord needs them,' and he will immediately let you take them."

⁴ This took place to fulfill the prophecy that said,

⁵ "Tell the people of Jerusalem,

'Look, your King is coming to you.

He is humble, riding on a donkey—

riding on a donkey's colt.'"

⁶ The two disciples did as Jesus commanded. ⁷ They

brought the donkey and the colt to him and threw their garments over the colt, and he sat on it.

⁸ Most of the crowd spread their garments on the road ahead of him, and others cut branches from the trees and spread them on the road. ⁹ Jesus was in the center of the procession, and the people all around him were shouting,

"Praise God for the Son of David!

Blessings on the one who comes in the name of the LORD!

Praise God in highest heaven!"

¹⁰ The entire city of Jerusalem was in an uproar as he entered. "Who is this?" they asked.

¹¹ And the crowds replied, "It's Jesus, the prophet from Nazareth in Galilee." (Matthew 21:1-11, NLT)

On this very day, Jerusalem was filled with people choosing their lambs for Passover. The focus was completely on selecting the perfect lamb. As Jesus rode into Jerusalem, the people called him out as the Messiah, but on this day, they unknowingly were indicating that He was the one that would provide everything the Messiah would provide, especially freedom from their captors. They were selecting their lamb, without even knowing it!

For thousands of years, the Jews referred back to the instructions God gave Moses in selecting the initial Passover lambs for sacrifice and used those instructions each year thereafter. The lamb had to meet the conditions in Exodus 12: "⁵ The animal you select must be a one-year-old male, either a sheep or a goat, with no defects."

This was vital to the plan of God, and the people's redemption from Egypt. The lamb had to be one-year-old male (the age coincides with innocence), a lamb with no defects (considered perfect).

This too, points to Jesus. One day, John the Baptist was baptizing in the Jordan River. As he was baptizing people, Jesus came down to the water, and immediately John said:

[29] ... "Look! The Lamb of God who takes away the sin of the world! (John 1:29, NLT)

Over and over the Bible refers to Jesus as the Lamb of God. In Revelations alone, he is referred to the LAMB of GOD twenty-nine times.

Throughout the New Testament, virtually every new testament writer makes the connection about Jesus being the LAMB of GOD...and Peter wrote that he was perfect:

[18] For you know that God paid a ransom to save you from the empty life you inherited from your ancestors. And it was not paid with mere gold or silver, which lose their value. [19] It was the precious blood of Christ, the sinless, spotless Lamb of God. [20] God chose him as your ransom long before the world began, but now in these last days he has been revealed for your sake. (1 Peter 1:18-20, NLT)

Jesus was the perfect lamb of God...and he was selected to be the sacrifice by God before the world began.

So, as Jesus is riding into Jerusalem, Jews are selecting a lamb to sacrifice...and Jesus, the TRUE Lamb of God, selected by God, and unknowingly by the people, would be sacrificed in a few days.

For the Jews in Jerusalem, the were told to keep the lamb for four days to examine the lamb to ensure it was perfect. If it had a flaw found during that four-day period, it was not fit for sacrifice.

Jesus, the LAMB of GOD...was also kept for four days from selection day until sacrifice day.

Between the Day of Selection until the day of crucifixion, Jesus was questioned by the Gentiles (the Romans), The Chief Priests, scribes and elders, and the Pharisees and Sadducees.

He was questioned in Luke 20:1-8 where they questioned His authority by asking Jesus, 'Just who do you think you are?'

Again in Luke 20:19-2 they tried to trap him into defying governmental authority, asking him, 'Who do you think is ruler?'

He was questioned by Roman authorities, but none could find any flaw in him. In fact, he was declared innocent. Prior to his crucifixion, the rulers said, 'we can find no fault with this man!'

During this selection period, every effort was made to ensure that the lamb was found to be perfect, and Jesus was found to be without fault.

Once the selection was completed and the four days were over, the next step occurred:

[6] "Take special care of this chosen animal until the evening of the fourteenth day of this first month. Then the whole assembly of the community of Israel must slaughter their lamb or young goat at twilight. (Exodus 12:6, NLT)

Because the Jews viewed each new day beginning at dusk

(sunset), and ending at dusk, that would make the timeline of events different than our western custom of when a day begins and ends. In the United States, and most Western nations, we view midnight as the time the day changes.

On the fourteenth day, which began when the sun set, was the moment the Passover was being prepared for slaughter.

It was evening on the fourteenth day (which began the fourteenth day) that the disciples and Jesus met for a Passover meal.

[17] On the first day of the Festival of Unleavened Bread, the disciples came to Jesus and asked, "Where do you want us to prepare the Passover meal for you?"

[18] "As you go into the city," he told them, "you will see a certain man. Tell him, 'The Teacher says: My time has come, and I will eat the Passover meal with my disciples at your house.' " [19] So the disciples did as Jesus told them and prepared the Passover meal there. (Matthew 26:17-19, NLT)

Now, when God gave Moses instructions for the Passover meal, it was as follows:

[6] "Take special care of this chosen animal until the evening of the fourteenth day of this first month. Then the whole assembly of the community of Israel must slaughter their lamb or young goat at twilight. [7] They are to take some of the blood and smear it on the sides and top of the doorframes of the houses where they eat the animal. [8] That same night they must roast the meat over a fire and eat it along with bitter salad greens and bread made without yeast. [9] Do not eat any of the meat raw or boiled in water. The whole animal—including the

head, legs, and internal organs—must be roasted over a fire.
[10] Do not leave any of it until the next morning. Burn whatever is not eaten before morning. (Exodus 12:6-10, NLT)

The instructions that God gave Moses was that all of the lamb had to be gone...nothing left.

Why?

God did not want the people to start worshipping a lamb, somehow thinking that animal was their deliverer out of Egypt, or that the blood of that lamb was sufficient to be worthy of worship.

When there's nothing left, there's nothing left to worship.

There WOULD be a lamb worthy of worship, but not the lamb Moses and the Jews sacrificed on the night of the first Passover.

It wasn't the lamb that Moses killed that set them free from Egypt, it was the LORD.

We can fall into the same trap. We can receive a blessing and because of that blessing, start trusting the blessing instead of trusting God.

For example, we might be blessed with money, and because of that money, turn it against our relationship with God. What was once a blessing, then turns into trips, toys, temporary pleasures and, before long, what was worshipped is now gone.

As my friend Al says, "Don't take the blessings God has given and turn around and use them against God."

There is a subtle thing that happens that if we are not careful in honoring God with our things...and with our money...because eventually, there will be nothing left. Nothing left to worship. God will insist on it.

When Jesus met with the disciples for the Passover meal, it was on the fourteenth evening, and the night before crucifixion. At that meal, there was no mention of the Passover Lamb, or them eating lamb. Why?

I believe it was for two reasons: First, lambs would be sacrificed in the morning and afternoon on the fourteenth day (which was the morning and afternoon after the Passover Meal). Remember, in the eyes of the Jews, this is still the same day.

Second, Jesus was the lamb that would be slain, so, the connection would not be made with an animal but with the elements on that Passover table, namely the bread and wine.

²⁶ As they were eating, Jesus took some bread and blessed it. Then he broke it in pieces and gave it to the disciples, saying, "Take this and eat it, for this is my body."

²⁷ And he took a cup of wine and gave thanks to God for it. He gave it to them and said, "Each of you drink from it, ²⁸ for this is my blood, which confirms the covenant between God and his people. It is poured out as a sacrifice to forgive the sins of many. ²⁹ Mark my words—I will not drink wine again until the day I drink it new with you in my Father's Kingdom."

³⁰ Then they sang a hymn and went out to the Mount of Olives. (Matthew 26:26-30, NLT)

Jesus used the elements to begin a new celebration for

believers, a distinction between His body...connected with bread...and His blood, connected with the blood of a new and better covenant.

After the meal, Jesus traveled to the garden of Gethsemane, while he prayed, he was betrayed and arrested. At about 2 a.m., Jesus began the first of six trials. The first three were religious trials before religious authorities: Annas, Caiaphas, and the Sanhedrin. The final three were before Roman authorities: Pilate, Herod, and then back to Pilate.

After the six trials, Jesus was beaten, a crown of thorns was placed on his head, and he was led to crucifixion.

This is Passover. At the very moment he was first nailed to the cross, not far away, the very first Jewish worshippers were lined up to sacrifice lambs to the Lord. For hundreds of years, it started at that very hour.

At noon, a daily sacrifice is offered to the Lord, and this coincides with the sky turning black when Jesus was crucified.

At 3 p.m., the people of Israel are called to begin sacrifices of their Passover lamb...it was at that moment, the call to sacrifice was announced by a shofar. So, in Jerusalem, a loud Shofar sounded...and the people knew two things. One, that it was the ninth hour (3 p.m.) and two, the call to sacrifice their lambs for Passover was to begin.

This trumpet would call people to sacrifice their lamb or goat in preparation to apply the blood to their door posts. This is what the Bible records happening on Passover when Jesus was crucified:

[45] At noon, darkness fell across the whole land until three

o'clock. [46] At about three o'clock, Jesus called out with a loud voice, "Eli, Eli, lema sabachthani?" which means "My God, my God, why have you abandoned me?" (Matthew 27:45–46, NLT)

How did the writer know it was 3 p.m.? It was probably because he heard the shofar calling the people to sacrifice their lamb. He heard it…and then, this is what the Bible says:

[47] Some of the bystanders misunderstood and thought he was calling for the prophet Elijah. [48] One of them ran and filled a sponge with sour wine, holding it up to him on a reed stick so he could drink. [49] But the rest said, "Wait! Let's see whether Elijah comes to save him."

[50] Then Jesus shouted out again, and he released his spirit. [51] At that moment the curtain in the sanctuary of the Temple was torn in two, from top to bottom. The earth shook, rocks split apart, [52] and tombs opened. The bodies of many godly men and women who had died were raised from the dead. (Matthe 27:47-52, NLT)

On that day, as the people were sacrificing their Passover lambs, Jesus was being crucified for their sins.

Let's go back to the original Passover.

Moses gave the instructions for every home to apply the blood to the doorposts and to partake all of the sacrifice, leaving nothing behind. Nothing left. It's all or nothing.

They applied the blood and during the night, the death angel went throughout the land, and if the death angel saw the blood on the doorposts, then the house was saved. Literally, the people would not die. Then they would be able to go free and would be able to travel to a land that God had set aside just for them. A land he said flowed with milk and honey, a beautiful dreamlike eternal home.

But, if the blood was not applied, the first born would die. Death would rule and reign! It was not enough to have a sacrifice without the application of the sacrificial blood to the doorposts.

What a powerful picture of what Jesus did for us!

We were bound our captors, suffering from the plagues of the gods of this world…bound to slavery…and then one day, someone tells us that there is a remedy. That an amazing God has come to set us free. He has come to take us out of bondage and take us to an amazing place that he designed just for us.

All we have to do is find the remedy through a relationship with Jesus. He would apply His blood to our lives…to the doorpost of our hearts…and it would mark us as His own. This very act would set us apart from everyone else. We had the remedy AND the relationship….

Death could not touch us, like it would everyone else. And through the blood of Jesus, we would be set free from our captors.

God told the people of Israel, "when I see the blood, I will pass over you. The plague of death will not touch you when I strike the land." (Exodus 12:13)

Scripture tells us that through the blood of Jesus, we have redemption. Revelations says we are made overcomers by the blood of the lamb…the Bible tells us he can wash us with his blood…that we are saved by His blood…and that His blood is the only cleansing agent that can wash away our sin.

Over and over again, scriptures declare that because of Jesus' death on the cross, our sins are taken away (Matthew 26:28), we dwell in Christ, and Christ dwells in us (John 6:56), it satisfies the payment we owed because of our sin (Romans 3:25), it saves us from judgment (Romans 5:9), it redeems us (Ephesians 1:7; 1 Peter 1:18-19, Revelations 5:9), it brings us near to God (Ephesians 2:13), it brings us forgiveness (Colossians 1:14), it causes us to overcome the devil (Revelation 12:11), and because of it, we can boldly come into God's presence and ask God to meet our needs (Hebrews 10:19).

There are dozens more scriptures that share more about the sacrifice of Jesus on the cross and how much better it was than the original Passover lamb.

That original lamb was the means that God used to set the people free from Egypt, but the Lamb of God, JESUS CHRIST, is the means through which we have eternal salvation. His death set us free from sin, gave us access to God, established a relationship with God, and that relationship frees us from our sin. The only thing we have to do is ask God to apply that remedy to our lives, and then, begin a relationship with Him.

Hundreds of years before Jesus came, God established in men's minds that there was a remedy to a death angel, and an opportunity to have a relationship with God. But even before time began, God knew that we would need a Savior. We would need a perfect lamb to pay a price that we could not pay to earn our freedom, and because Jesus came and died, we have an opportunity to know this Amazing God.

But it does not stop there!

CHAPTER 4

———➤ ◆ ◀———

MIGHTY GOD

God may sometimes lead you to the edge of your ability after a great victory, which is what he did for the Jews.

The victory was powerful, but distant. Let's face it: none of the Jews experienced anything the night the death angel passed over their house. They did not experience death, no weeping in the camp, nothing but quiet.

***Sometimes peace is as much of a
miracle as a mountain moved!***

Occasionally, we are confronted with the real possibility that if our child had not made a mess and delayed our travel, we would have been in a life-altering accident. If our spouse would not have been slow in getting dressed, we could have died. It's not often that we see the passive miracles around us, but I am convinced that like the Jews, we have much to be thankful for even if the tragedy was distant and we were spared.

Everything God did was distant to the people of Israel up until the time of the plagues. As far as we know, Moses and Aaron did not go to the people of Israel and tell them what God was going to do to the Egyptians. We don't know if they were warned of any of the plagues that would affect them, or if they knew beforehand about the gnats, flies, death of the livestock, or the plague of darkness that would touch Egypt in a profound way, but leave them in peace.

He did tell the people about the Passover, and God's intent to deliver one more plague.

God did, and the people only heard about the horror in a distant region. But even then, the children of Israel did not get it.

So, the people of Israel had witnessed from a distance, and knew that their first-born was alive because of the hand of God...but it would have likely been surreal up until the Passover.

It's almost like a process where God reveals Himself in steps due to the difficulty of revealing a God so complex and powerful, that He must reveal Himself a little at a time. God tells Moses that He is the I AM. Plagues come and God touches the Jews, but only with the first few plagues. Then, the rest of plagues are only rumors the Jews heard, because it never came to their house. Most plagues did not affect them.

After God sent the death angel, Pharaoh had enough and he ordered the Jews to leave.

[37] That night the people of Israel left Rameses and started for Succoth. There were about 600,000 men, plus all the women and children. [38] A rabble of non-Israelites went with them, along with great flocks and herds of livestock. [39] For bread they baked flat cakes from the dough without yeast they had brought from Egypt. It was made without yeast because the people were driven out of Egypt in such a hurry that they had no time to prepare the bread or other food. [40] The people of Israel had lived in Egypt for 430 years. [41] In fact, it was on the last day of the 430th year that all the Lord's forces left the

land. [42] On this night the Lord kept his promise to bring his people out of the land of Egypt. So this night belongs to him, and it must be commemorated every year by all the Israelites, from generation to generation. (Exodus 12:37–42, NLT)

God kept his promise and on the very last day of the 430th year they left the land. This is an incredible example of the timeless truth: God is always on time. But the time is HIS TIME.

Whatever you are going through that is time sensitive, make sure you give it to God, and let Him worry about the timing. He has time and eternity in His hand, and moves according to His powerful time frame.

For the Egyptians, their first-born were being buried at the same time the people of Israel were dedicating their first-born to the Lord. The Jewish first born lived because the parents obeyed and now they belonged to the Lord.

[3] So Moses said to the people, "This is a day to remember forever—the day you left Egypt, the place of your slavery. Today the Lord has brought you out by the power of His mighty hand. (Exodus 13:3, NLT)

What a powerful statement: Today the Lord has brought you out by the power of his mighty hand. They were not brought out by the power of their sacrifice, but by the power of God.

This AMAZING GOD was demonstrating HIS MIGHTY POWER.

On our road of life, as we walk the journey God purposed for us, He always wants to show us more than a passive view of

Himself. He does not want us to know Him as a God of yesterday, one that long ago did mighty works, but that those days are over.

There are some that believe that. They believe that God used to do things…they believe that God is not doing miracles today.

That somehow the days of God performing MIGHTY deeds are over.

I want to make a declaration to you today. God is still God and He has not stopped doing miracles. He is still breaking chains, still saving lost souls, still healing broken bodies, still moving powerfully in the lives of anyone who will believe in Him. Jesus is no longer in the grave. Some act like that when Jesus died, so did His power. The same power that raised Christ from the dead is living in you.

You may not be experiencing God's miracle-working power in your life right now, but that does not mean He can not…or will not…He just HAS NOT… yet.

I believe this: That all along your journey of life, God is revealing Himself to you in a variety of ways. He wants you to know Him in every way. But, don't discount the possibility that sometime today, or tomorrow, or next week, or right now, somebody is about to experience God's mighty power. He will deliver you by His MIGHTY HAND. There is a miracle in the making for somebody reading this today.

Now, there is a thing about this part of 'delivering by His

Mighty Hand.'

[17] When Pharaoh finally let the people go, God did not lead them along the main road that runs through Philistine territory, even though that was the shortest route to the Promised Land. God said, "If the people are faced with a battle, they might change their minds and return to Egypt." [18] So God led them in a roundabout way through the wilderness toward the Red Sea. Thus the Israelites left Egypt like an army ready for battle. (Exodus 13:17-18, NLT)

So, God was at work leading the people of Israel, leading them 'like an army ready for battle' but the Lord knew they were not ready for a battle. They were chickens, scared and inept at military battle.

I am not making light of them, because you and I can do the same thing. When faced with insurmountable odds and God calls us to a step of faith, sometimes we can reply to the voice of God by saying, "I can never do that." In that moment, we are intimidated to step out in faith because we are afraid.

Sometimes God will take us around a problem because He knows we are unable to fight it. Other times, he will take us through the problem, not because we are ready, but because we are ready to call on Him for help. The Jews were not there yet, but soon, the challenge would be issued.

[20] The Israelites left Succoth and camped at Etham on the edge of the wilderness. [21] The Lord went ahead of them. He guided them during the day with a pillar of cloud, and he provided light at night with a pillar of fire. This allowed them to travel by day or by night. [22] And the Lord did not remove

the pillar of cloud or pillar of fire from its place in front of the people. (Exodus 13:17–22, NLT)

What an Amazing God, who provided air conditioning for the daytime and when the night air cooled in the desert, He provided fire by night.

After leading them to Etham, God began a divine setup. One that took the people into harms way for the sole purpose of showing that He was God and that they could trust Him completely.

Then the Lord gave these instructions to Moses: ² "Order the Israelites to turn back and camp by Pi-hahiroth between Migdol and the sea. Camp there along the shore, across from Baal-zephon. ³ Then Pharaoh will think, 'The Israelites are confused. They are trapped in the wilderness!' ⁴ And once again I will harden Pharaoh's heart, and he will chase after you. I have planned this in order to display my glory through Pharaoh and his whole army. After this the Egyptians will know that I am the Lord!" So the Israelites camped there as they were told. (Exodus 14:1–4, NLT)

God wanted to reveal to the Jews that He was the one that makes a way, even when their back was against a wall. But God was also setting up the enemy for failure. There is a powerful template this story provides for your life. When we follow God, He will set you up for victory, and at the same time, He will set the enemy up for failure. Your enemy (Satan) will be emboldened, he will see you and surmise that you are in complete confusion. He may even whisper doubts to your mind, and taunt you for believing God or His Word. Those taunts will continue and it will look as if God is nowhere around, and that you are about to lose the largest battle in your life. At that one moment, Satan will overstep himself.

This is a spiritual principle. When your enemy comes in, like a flood the Spirit of the Lord will raise a standard against the enemy. (Isaiah 59:19)

Your enemy will overstep himself. He will take the moment when you feel overwhelmed and stuck between the Red Sea and the approaching enemy and do his very best to stir up fear in your heart. It will almost feel like your problems have intensified, which is Satan's tactic to bring you to doubt God's goodness, or to cause fear to overwhelm your peace. When this happens, it is very possible that God Himself has established a divine setup to destroy the enemy and to rescue you from the oncoming onslaught.

If you are following the Lord, just like the Jews were, know that He will lead you to complex and impossible places to show you His mighty power. It is all a part of His plan of revealing Himself to you in your trial!

Exodus 14 continues: [5] When word reached the king of Egypt that the Israelites had fled, Pharaoh and his officials changed their minds. "What have we done, letting all those Israelite slaves get away?" they asked. [6] So Pharaoh harnessed his chariot and called up his troops. [7] He took with him 600 of Egypt's best chariots, along with the rest of the chariots of Egypt, each with its commander. [8] The Lord hardened the heart of Pharaoh, the king of Egypt, so he chased after the people of Israel, who had left with fists raised in defiance. [9] The Egyptians chased after them with all the forces in Pharaoh's army—all his horses and chariots, his charioteers, and his troops. The Egyptians caught up with the people of Israel as they were camped beside the shore near Pi-hahiroth, across from Baal-zephon. (Exodus 14:5-9, NLT)

It's not about a remedy, now it is about a relationship built on trust.

[10] As Pharaoh approached, the people of Israel looked up and panicked when they saw the Egyptians overtaking them. They cried out to the Lord, [11] and they said to Moses, "Why did you bring us out here to die in the wilderness? Weren't there enough graves for us in Egypt? What have you done to us? Why did you make us leave Egypt? [12] Didn't we tell you this would happen while we were still in Egypt? We said, 'Leave us alone! Let us be slaves to the Egyptians. It's better to be a slave in Egypt than a corpse in the wilderness!' " (Exodus 14:10-12, NLT)

Their back was against the wall, and that was exactly God's plan.

[13] But Moses told the people, "Don't be afraid. Just stand still and watch the Lord rescue you today. The Egyptians you see today will never be seen again. [14] The Lord himself will fight for you. Just stay calm." (Exodus 14:13-14, NLT)

My friend, Gary Sapp once said,

If God brings you to it, He will bring you through it!

It's usually at this point in our life story that we resolve to never find ourselves in such a predicament. We fear, and find

God's power, but the stress is too great and we would prefer a stress-free life. The faithful follower of Christ may never truly find such a place, where we are not called to deeper faith, greater trust than before. For it is such a place that brings about stress, but also the very place we grow to deeper levels in God. The levels He calls us to every single day.

[15] Then the Lord said to Moses, "Why are you crying out to me? Tell the people to get moving! [16] Pick up your staff and raise your hand over the sea. Divide the water so the Israelites can walk through the middle of the sea on dry ground. (Exodus 14:15, NLT)

Moses should've known by now that it was going to be big. God asks Moses, "Why are you crying out to me?"

That is a legitimate question. For a few months, God had performed over twelve miracles, turned water to blood, produced more frogs than anyone could count, created gnats from dust, biting flies by the billions, brought darkness so thick one could feel it, and then, used blood from a lamb to deflect a death angel's destruction. The question was a great question from an Amazing God. He had already shown Himself powerful, so this was nothing.

That problem is shared by you and me. Our experience through life continues to show God's power and provision, and yet, in the crisis we still fret.

Our courage is only as strong as our recollection, and mostly, we have spiritual dementia when it comes to the exploits of God on our behalf.

It gets back to the fact that it's all about a relationship. "Why are you crying out to me?"

If 'crying out to God' is what you mostly do, then it might be time to get moving, pick up your staff, raise up your hand, and believe God for a miracle. Now would be a great time to stop fretting and get moving on with God.

We have to be careful while 'crying out.' We may simply want God to do something for us that requires no commitment on our part. We might want magic instead of a miracle. We want God on the stage, doing the incredible things for us, while we sit back and applaud when it meets our definition of amazing. Miracles are not magic shows, but opportunities to partner with God to see how amazing He really is.

If you want a remedy without a relationship, you will find that as a follower of God, there will be a time when God won't let you off that easy. He will bring impossible situations your way to force you from the "God is like Santa Claus" mentality into saying, "God is Amazing; His wonders are too numerous to recount."

Scripture declares such a scenario:

17 And I will harden the hearts of the Egyptians, and they will charge in after the Israelites. My great glory will be displayed through Pharaoh and his troops, his chariots, and his charioteers. 18 When my glory is displayed through them, all Egypt will see my glory and know that I am the Lord!" (Exodus 14:17-18, NLT)

God was not done with Egypt. He wanted them to know

He is God. He wanted them to see His glory. It is almost as if God had been dealing with Egypt longer than just during the plagues. It's almost as if God started dealing with Egypt when Joseph came to lead during the famine, and for four hundred and thirty years, He showed them His grace and His power, but they continued to trust in their gods, and ignored the ONE TRUE God. After a while, the opportunity of grace ended.

While God's grace is unmerited,
it can also be unwelcomed,
And the potential recipients can lose out on the
opportunity of God's grace in their lives.

I believe He does the same for us. He works with us time and again, but if we keep refusing, we will one day see His glory and power, but it will be against us and not on our behalf. As it was not a favorable outcome for Egypt:

¹⁹ Then the angel of God, who had been leading the people of Israel, moved to the rear of the camp. The pillar of cloud also moved from the front and stood behind them. ²⁰ The cloud settled between the Egyptian and Israelite camps. As darkness fell, the cloud turned to fire, lighting up the night. But the Egyptians and Israelites did not approach each other all night. (Exodus 14:19-20, NLT)

When God is in charge, look out. Even your enemy will be amazed at God's activity.

²¹ Then Moses raised his hand over the sea, and the Lord opened up a path through the water with a strong east wind.

The wind blew all that night, turning the seabed into dry land.
²² So the people of Israel walked through the middle of the sea
on dry ground, with walls of water on each side! (Exodus
14:21-22, NLT)

God is not about a lead up, or some type of dramatic build,
because sometimes it is not about a moment. Yes, he brings
moments, but sometimes He wants you to see His power in
more than a moment. He wants you to know that He is God
over time and eternity.

He has the power to do the AMAZING THINGS in our
lives and a simple raising of the staff was enough for God to
move in this situation. We sometimes think it will take
Hollywood movie moment, where in dramatic fashion, Moses
raises his staff, tells the millions of Jews to 'wait for it, wait for
it,' and then declares with a changed voice and great authority,
"Stand still and see the salvation of the Lord," and then,
BOOM, the miracle happens.

It may be that way, but do not believe the lie that God is
about a dramatic pause, or a powerful build up. He is about
His purpose and I believe, our good!

A simple raise of the hand and then the Jewish people
walked through the Red Sea on dry ground. How amazing is
that?

At some places, the Red Sea is over 7,000 feet deep and
over 100 miles wide.

The place where the people walked through the Red Sea
was not that deep or wide. I know, I just downloaded a 'deep
and wide' playlist in your brain.

Think about well over one and a half million Jews with animals walking through the Red Sea during the night, on a path that was nearly eight miles wide and one thousand feet deep at the location the Jews crossed.

They walked through the night…²³ Then the Egyptians—all of Pharaoh's horses, chariots, and charioteers—chased them into the middle of the sea. ²⁴ But just before dawn the Lord looked down on the Egyptian army from the pillar of fire and cloud, and he threw their forces into total confusion. ²⁵ He twisted their chariot wheels, making their chariots difficult to drive. "Let's get out of here—away from these Israelites!" the Egyptians shouted. "The Lord is fighting for them against Egypt!" (Exodus 14:23-25, NLT)

Your enemy will do the same thing. He will chase you to the end but if you are following God, but you have to know, God will not let the enemy come near. It starts with relationship and God is all about that relationship. It is moments like these that Psalm 91 comes to mind, as it relates to where the Jewish people are in this story, and where we find ourselves in life:

Psalm 91

¹ Those who live in the shelter of the Most High
    will find rest in the shadow of the Almighty.
² This I declare about the Lord:
He alone is my refuge, my place of safety;
    he is my God, and I trust him.
³ For he will rescue you from every trap
    and protect you from deadly disease.

⁴ He will cover you with his feathers.
      He will shelter you with his wings.
      His faithful promises are your armor and protection.
⁵ Do not be afraid of the terrors of the night,
      nor the arrow that flies in the day.
⁶ Do not dread the disease that stalks in darkness,
      nor the disaster that strikes at midday.
⁷ Though a thousand fall at your side,
      though ten thousand are dying around you,
      these evils will not touch you.
⁸ Just open your eyes,
      and see how the wicked are punished.
⁹ If you make the Lord your refuge,
      if you make the Most High your shelter,
¹⁰ no evil will conquer you;
      no plague will come near your home.
¹¹ For he will order his angels
      to protect you wherever you go.
¹² They will hold you up with their hands
      so you won't even hurt your foot on a stone.
¹³ You will trample upon lions and cobras;
      you will crush fierce lions and serpents under your feet!
¹⁴ The Lord says, "I will rescue those who love me.
      I will protect those who trust in my name.
¹⁵ When they call on me, I will answer;
      I will be with them in trouble.
      I will rescue and honor them.
¹⁶ I will reward them with a long life
      and give them my salvation." (Psalm 91, NLT)

The fear of the approaching army probably scared the Jews

like no other time. Just like such a picture would strike terror in our heart. But, the same God that called the Jews to this place is the same God of power that can deal with the enemy.

26 When all the Israelites had reached the other side, the Lord said to Moses, "Raise your hand over the sea again. Then the waters will rush back and cover the Egyptians and their chariots and charioteers." 27 So as the sun began to rise, Moses raised his hand over the sea, and the water rushed back into its usual place. The Egyptians tried to escape, but the Lord swept them into the sea. 28 Then the waters returned and covered all the chariots and charioteers—the entire army of Pharaoh. Of all the Egyptians who had chased the Israelites into the sea, not a single one survived.

29 But the people of Israel had walked through the middle of the sea on dry ground, as the water stood up like a wall on both sides. 30 That is how the Lord rescued Israel from the hand of the Egyptians that day. And the Israelites saw the bodies of the Egyptians washed up on the seashore. (Exodus 14:26-30, NLT)

God does not just set a table before you in the presence of your enemies. He also takes your enemy to the middle of the sea, confuses their horses, messes up their rims, and destroys them completely, right before your eyes.

It is good to be reminded that your true enemy is not a boss, an ex-spouse, or your next-door neighbor. The enemy that is common among every human is the eternal enemy that seeks to steal, kill, and destroy. He is referred to as Satan or the devil and his goal is to keep you from the relationship God wants to have with you. He knows if you truly get into a deep, meaningful relationship with God, he is toast.

[31] When the people of Israel saw the mighty power that the Lord had unleashed against the Egyptians, they were filled with awe before him. They put their faith in the Lord and in his servant Moses. (Exodus 14:31, NLT)

They went from seeing an AMAZING GOD…to seeing HIS MIGHTY POWER, to putting their faith in the Lord. I wish that would have changed them. While it says that they put their faith in the Lord and in his servant Moses, that statement would be tried severely in the future.

As with the Jews, God will bring you to the edge of nowhere with the enemy swiftly approaching, and nowhere to run to show you His power and to reveal an aspect of WHO HE IS. He wants you to see His MIGHTY POWER and to know this AMAZING GOD. That is always the aim.

I believe that one of the best days of your life
will be the day when you fully realize
that God has always had your best interest at heart!

CHAPTER 5

---◆◆◆---

A GOD WHO IS

There is a powerful moment in a victory that embeds itself in our minds. In a sporting event, it may be the play that turned the momentum our direction. In life, it could be the 'right on time' moment that God comes through. You know the moment: When you are out of hope and out of cash, a check arrives at just the precise moment, and then, in epic fashion you make it to the bank with minutes to spare. Do you remember those times? Me neither.

For a moment we do, and the celebration decibel level is at its highest.

Imagine running from a quickly approaching foe that is armed with every military tool, with numbers that would overwhelm any other army. And then, in epic fashion, God closes the route. Not with a barricade, but with billions and billions of gallons of water rushing and crushing the enemy. This is what the Jews witnessed first hand.

The enemy that brought such terror only moments before was dead, and the bodies of the Egyptian army were washing up on the banks of the Red Sea as a tribute to the power of God.

The celebration for the Jews matched the victory:

Exodus 15 says:

Then Moses and the people of Israel sang this song to the Lord:
  "I will sing to the Lord,
    for he has triumphed gloriously;

he has hurled both horse and rider
    into the sea.
² The Lord is my strength and my song;
    he has given me victory.
This is my God, and I will praise him—
    my father's God, and I will exalt him!
³ The Lord is a warrior;
    Yahweh is his name!
⁴ Pharaoh's chariots and army
    he has hurled into the sea.
The finest of Pharaoh's officers
    are drowned in the Red Sea.
⁵ The deep waters gushed over them;
    they sank to the bottom like a stone.
⁶ "Your right hand, O Lord,
    is glorious in power.
Your right hand, O Lord,
    smashes the enemy.
⁷ In the greatness of your majesty,
    you overthrow those who rise against you.
You unleash your blazing fury;
    it consumes them like straw.
⁸ At the blast of your breath,
    the waters piled up!
The surging waters stood straight like a wall;
    in the heart of the sea the deep waters became hard.
⁹ "The enemy boasted, 'I will chase them
    and catch up with them.
I will plunder them
    and consume them.
I will flash my sword;
    my powerful hand will destroy them.'

¹⁰ But you blew with your breath,
and the sea covered them.
They sank like lead
in the mighty waters.
¹¹ "Who is like you among the gods, O Lord—
glorious in holiness,
awesome in splendor,
performing great wonders?
¹² You raised your right hand,
and the earth swallowed our enemies.
¹³ "With your unfailing love you lead
the people you have redeemed.
In your might, you guide them
to your sacred home.
¹⁴ The peoples hear and tremble;
anguish grips those who live in Philistia.
¹⁵ The leaders of Edom are terrified;
the nobles of Moab tremble.
All who live in Canaan melt away;
¹⁶ terror and dread fall upon them.
The power of your arm
makes them lifeless as stone
until your people pass by, O Lord,
until the people you purchased pass by.
¹⁷ You will bring them in and plant them on your own
mountain— the place, O Lord, reserved for your own
dwelling, the sanctuary, O Lord, that your hands have
established.
¹⁸ The Lord will reign forever and ever!"
¹⁹ When Pharaoh's horses, chariots, and charioteers rushed
into the sea, the Lord brought the water crashing down on
them. But the people of Israel had walked through the middle

of the sea on dry ground!

²⁰ Then Miriam the prophet, Aaron's sister, took a tambourine and led all the women as they played their tambourines and danced.

²¹ And Miriam sang this song: "Sing to the Lord, for he has triumphed gloriously; he has hurled both horse and rider into the sea." (Exodus 15:1-21, NLT)

The people were rejoicing over their deliverance. God's desire was to reveal Himself to the people of Israel as their deliverer. He nailed it. He established, once again, He was the God who sets captives free. The God who can do anything. The God with all power, and might, and the God who delivers.

At the onset, God could have just killed every Egyptian and led the children of Israel straight to the Promised Land. He could have done that in a period of about a month, but the people would not have known God. They would have only benefited from God's actions but missed the opportunity to know God in more than a one dimensional way.

God will sometimes lead you to uncomfortable places, bad spaces, or sad moments to show Himself real to you. He may put your back to the wall so you can see that He delivers His people. His goal is to prepare you for heaven and that is accomplished through gaining greater revelation of who God is - not just seeing what He can do.

That is why I believe we are looking at it all wrong. Every trial, every storm, every illness, every pain, everything that you are going through looks like one thing, and the more you focus on that one thing, framed the wrong way, it clouds your perspective. You get it wrong. I get it wrong.

You don't see it but your trial that God sent is more about your relationship with Him than you know.

The Jews now had the profound understanding that God could deliver. He was more than a delivering God, though, and He desired the people to know Him in greater ways!

Scripture bears this out: "Then Moses led the people of Israel away from the Red Sea, and they moved out into the desert of Shur." (Exodus 15:22, NLT)

This route would take them south, not east. They needed to travel east to get to the Promised Land, but God led them south for a reason.

They traveled in this desert for three days without finding any water.

Just a few days prior, they were in a great place, celebrating God's delivering power. At this point, they had traveled three days in the desert without water. They were very thirsty. When they came to the oasis of Marah, the water was too bitter to drink. So they called the place Marah (which means "bitter"). (Exodus 15:23, NLT)

Marah is usually identified with Ain Hawarah, a site many miles inland from the Suez Canal. Ain Hawarah's waters are notoriously brackish. [8]

---

[8] Kaiser, W. C., Jr. (1990). Exodus. In F. E. Gaebelein (Ed.), The Expositor's Bible Commentary: Genesis, Exodus, Leviticus, Numbers

Describing the well at Marah, Edward Robinson says: "The well is six or eight feet in diameter, and the water about two feet deep. Its taste is unpleasant, saltish, and somewhat bitter ... The Arabs ... consider it as the worst water in all these regions."[9]

The water was bitter because it had a high content of sodium chloride, calcium, and magnesium. The high levels of such particular minerals would make the water beautiful and clear, but oily to the touch.

The combination of minerals would have caused intestinal cramps and diarrhea to anyone drinking from its source. It was a powerful laxative. No wonder the Arabs considered it the worst water in the entire region!

The people complained bitterly about the water. I believe they complained about the taste as well as the effects of the water.

Notice what is next:

[24] Then the people complained and turned against Moses. "What are we going to drink?" they demanded. [25] So Moses cried out to the Lord for help, and the Lord showed him a piece of wood. Moses threw it into the water, and this made the water good to drink. (Exodus 15:24-25, NLT)

According to some, this species of wood had a sap that caused the water to become sweet. Maybe it was simply

---

(Vol. 2, p. 398). Grand Rapids, MI: Zondervan Publishing House.

[9] (Biblical Researches in Palestine 3 vols. [Boston: Crocker and Brewster, 1857–60], 2:96)

obedience to God that made the water sweet. We don't know that this sweetness did not alleviate the effects of the water, but it certainly made the water taste better.

It is very possible that the effects of the water had already met its intended goal of cleansing the body from the diseases of Egypt.

It was there at Marah that the Lord set before them the following decree as a standard to test their faithfulness to him. [26] He said, "If you will listen carefully to the voice of the Lord your God and do what is right in his sight, obeying his commands and keeping all his decrees, then I will not make you suffer any of the diseases I sent on the Egyptians; (Exodus 15:25-26, NLT)

Have you ever wondered, "What were the diseases God sent on the Egyptians?" There were many, but none more profound than four parasites that were typical in Egypt at that time.

There were four types of parasites that would have been very dangerous for the people of Israel as they walked through the desert on the way to the Promised Land. According to University College London, they were: Bill Har Zia, Guinea Worm, Round Worm, And Tape Worm.[10]

Symptoms of Bill Har Zia (schistosomiasis) are caused not by the worms themselves but by the body's reaction to the eggs. Eggs shed by the adult worms that do not pass out of the body

---

[10] http://www.ucl.ac.uk/museums-static/digitalegypt/age/disease.html

can become lodged in the intestine or bladder, causing inflammation or scarring. Children who are repeatedly infected can develop anemia, malnutrition, and learning difficulties. After years of infection, the parasite can also damage the liver, intestine, spleen, lungs, and bladder.

Complications of Guinea Worm can include a slight fever, itchy rash, nausea, vomiting, diarrhea, painful blisters, cellulitis (skin infection), boils, sepsis and septic arthritis, and even tetanus (lock jaw). If the worm breaks during removal it can cause intense inflammation as the remaining part of the dead worm starts to degrade inside the body. This causes more pain, swelling, and cellulitis.

Round worms can cause chronic cough, shortness of breath, abdominal pain, weight loss, and fatigue.
Tape worms can lead to serious complications, including blocking the intestine…and they can migrate to other parts of the body and cause damage to the liver, eyes, heart, and brain. These infections can be life-threatening.[11]

These parasites can potentially affect every part of the body: brain, eyes, mouth, ears and hearing, heart, lungs, blood, abdomen, lymph nodes, skin, hands, and feet. [12]

So, you can understand that these parasites would have affected the Jewish people for the rest of their lives. And if not healed from the parasites, they would have carried them to the

---

[11] http://www.webmd.com/digestive-disorders/tapeworms-in-humans
[12] https://umm.edu/health/medical/altmed/condition/roundworms

Promised Land. They would have infected their kids, and their grandkids and every generation thereafter.

Add to all of the symptoms the fact that the Jewish people were in the desert. The heat and fatigue from the heat, coupled with the symptoms from the parasites would likely overwhelm the immune system and certainly kill the weakest.

So, even though the water with the powerful laxative was uncomfortable for the people at the moment, it acted like a medicine to cleanse their system from the parasites they gained in Egypt.

Think about this: For three days, God let them get extremely thirsty and then took them to a pool of water with intention. He wanted to cleanse them from the diseases of their past lives, and reveal Himself as the healer of every disease they had known.

All of this was done so the people could be healthy but even more so, that the people would experience a dimension of God that they had never known.

They were sick and did not know it. They were taking medicine and did not know it. They needed healing and did not know it. They needed a greater revelation of God, and were about to receive it!

We are sick and we need healing too. We think of healing as mending a broken bone or opening blind eyes. God can do any of those things, but there are deeper maladies that God wants to heal.

We have parasites that destroy our lives. Our parasites are not in the food we have eaten or the water we drank in captivity. It is the things that happened to us, those things that deeply affect us today. We've been infected with the effects of our Egypt experience (life before we came to know God).

The things that happened to us in our Egypt experience can still deter us on our journey to the Promised Land.

Our Egypt experience is any thing at any time in our past when we did not have a revelation of God like we do today. Those experiences can include betrayal, jealousy, a crushed spirit, guilt, shame, unforgiveness, and bitterness.

Let's face it. We have all had the experience of Egypt, but some of our experiences are worse than others.

Some experiences may still affect us today. Sometimes that affect is PROFOUND. It not only marks our life; it touches relationships, jobs, our peace...everything.

Some take a huge toll in our lives today.

God led the Israelites to bitter waters to out the systems of those who were struggling with the parasites.

But it was bitter water.

That's exactly the taste that we experience emotionally when we think of those places in our lives that still affect us...they are bitter. As you read this, please understand that the goal is not to remind you of the bitter place, but to apply the healing sweetness of God's Word to that situation; the powerful presence of a loving God to your life, so that you can be healed.

God's desire in your life is to heal you of everything; to

cleanse you completely and to set you free, so that the rest of your journey can be healthy. He wants to reveal Himself to you today as the God who heals your life.

Here are some of the parasites that can affect us, and if we are not careful, they can affect and infect and affect us as well:

Jealousy

Proverbs 14:30 puts it this way:

> 30 A peaceful heart leads to a healthy body;
> jealousy is like cancer in the bones. [13]

What is jealousy?

Irish writer Elizabeth Bowen once wrote, "Jealousy is no more than feeling alone against smiling enemies." This simple statement sets a perfect scene in our minds of what jealousy feels like; others are happy, overtly joyful or secretly mocking, while we are left alone to look like a fool.

Jealousy can be like cancer especially when you are doing your very best but feeling like you are failing, while others seem to be walking through life without any effort. You try your best, but fail, and compared to them, you feel like a fool.

A Crushed Spirit

Proverbs 18:14 explains the overwhelming feeling of this parasite:

> The human spirit can endure a sick body,
> but who can bear a crushed spirit? (NLT)

---

[13] Tyndale House Publishers. (2013). Holy Bible: New Living Translation (Pr 14:30). Carol Stream, IL: Tyndale House Publishers.

That's why wisdom from Proverbs 4 warns us to:
²³ Guard your heart above all else,
    for it determines the course of your life. (NLT)
Sometimes the crushing of our spirit is life altering. It not only hurts our feelings, but also affects our spirit, and when the spirit is affected, the body is infected. That includes body, soul, and mind.

On churchlink.com, Steve Sutton wrote a blog that states: "There are those with extreme or severe damage to their spirit. These people are greatly incapacitated; dysfunctional with all manner of emotional, psychological, physical and social disabilities. These people are forced to crawl or need to be carried through life."

They have been severely wounded by someone in leadership. Jeremiah 23: 9 said as much:
"My heart is broken because of the false prophets,
    and my bones tremble.
I stagger like a drunkard,
    like someone overcome by wine,
because of the holy words
    the Lord has spoken against them." (NLT)

Jeremiah goes on to say his hurt was because the pastors, shepherds, and the prophets had failed in their leadership responsibility. Broken hearts and damaged spirits can also be brought about by the actions of our families, friends, and close acquaintances. Our own actions can also contribute.

Guilt

Guilt is also a parasite that can hinder our journey, and

there is a close association between unresolved guilt and physical and inner sickness.

Psalm 38:4-10 describes this parasite:

"My guilt has overwhelmed me like a burden too heavy to bear. My wounds fester...I am bowed down and brought very low...there is no health in my body...even the light has gone from my eyes." (NLT)

Steve Sutton explains, "Unresolved guilt makes our sins appear to be bigger than God's capacity to forgive."

Words/Criticism/Negativity

The old saying: "Sticks and stones may break my bones but words will never hurt me" is a dangerous lie. Words have spiritual values. They can create life in our spirit or they can produce death.

Throughout the book of Proverbs, we find the spiritual value of words. Chapter 18, verse 21 puts it this way, "The tongue has the power of life and death." (NLT)

"A lying tongue hates those it wounds and crushes, and a flattering mouth works ruin" (Proverbs 26:28 NLT)

Proverbs 15:4 states, "The tongue that brings healing is a tree of life but a deceitful tongue crushes the spirit." (NLT) Negativity and criticism can do more to wound and bruise the spirit than physical violence.

Abuse

Abuse is a parasite that affects every area of our lives, and it takes on three forms: verbal, physical, and sexual.

Verbal abuse is a sad part of our culture. It is all too common to hear people making fun of and ridiculing children, spouses and one another. In spite of the intention, this still hurts. It is particularly harmful when it comes from those who are close, who instead should support and uphold.

20 Their insults have broken my heart,
   and I am in despair.
If only one person would show some pity;
   if only one would turn and comfort me. (Psalm 69:20, NLT)

While verbal abuse typically affects us emotionally, physical abuse can wound us in ways deeper than a physical scar.

Physical abuse has a way of causing people to blame themselves for other people's violent tempers, or to look within for the cause of the abuse, rather than at the other person for inflicting the pain.

Sometimes the effects of sexual abuse can keep us from health in every area of our lives. It robs a victim of innocence and wounds the spirit. Intimacy issues grow from sexual abuse and can impair the victim long into their adult life.

There are other types of abuse that can lead us on a life long debilitated existence, such as mental or spiritual. Regardless of the type of abuse, all abuse becomes a powerful parasite that can leave a victim debilitated, unfulfilled, empty and frustrated.

Heartache

Sorrow or heartache is a damaging emotion that also acts like a parasite.

"A happy heart makes the face cheerful, but heartache (the KJV says "sorrow") crushes the spirit." (Proverbs 15:13 NLT)

Heartbreak is frequently the end product of an unfulfilled desire or craving. It's often the outcome of unrealistic expectations, where another person or some material pursuit is worshipped or idolized. It can also be the result of an inability to forgive and let go of those who have sinned against us.[14]

This area alone can trap individuals in a cycle of bitterness and unforgiveness, that is why I believe Jesus warned:

"So also my heavenly Father will deal with every one of you if you do not freely forgive your brother from your heart his offenses" (Matthew 18:35, NLT)

If parasites are allowed to remain, they will infect us with shame and guilt. That shame and guilt work together to create ripe conditions for addiction.

The reason God led the Jewish people to the bitter water was to heal them, not to destroy them. The same is true for us.

He used a name to reveal His power. The Jewish people had long known God as YAHWEH.

At the burning bush, God told Moses that he was "I AM, the self-existent, all-powerful One." It was in the desert, however, that the revelation God spoke to Moses and the Jewish people was greater, given in a way that is lost in our view of scripture.

He told them, "I AM the LORD who heals you."

Notice he says, "I AM" again the same construction of the

---

[14] (http://www.churchlink.com.au/churchlink/forum/broken_heart.html)

I AM phrase he told Moses at the burning bush. He says, "I AM the LORD..." which is YAWEH (we would typically say, JEHOVAH).

And then He says, "...who heals." That is where we miss the power of scripture through translation.

We sometimes view God's power the same way we view our occupation. For example, someone may say, "I am a pipe fitter, and I am a member of the pipefitter's union 121. That's what I do."

Once retired, that same person would say, "I was a pipe fitter, and I am still a member of pipefitters union 121. I have a great pension, live in Florida, and make sure my right turn signal is blinking on my car at all times."

He might even say, "From time to time, I get together with my pipe fitting friends and talk about the good old days when I used to fit pipes."

In other words, he means, "I used to do that, but I have retired."

That's the way some view God's declaration of His power to heal: As if it is a job that God once did, but now He has retired from healing because no one needs healing today, or more importantly, no one needs a better revelation of who God is today.

The Hebrew word for heal is the word Rapha. It is a verb, indicating action or a state of being. It is a Qal, which is a linguistic term in the Hebrew language meaning it connects the verb to the subject; it is a participle which means it has characteristics as both a verb and an adjective; it is singular, which means it comes from one person; it is active which means that it is current, with the potential to always be current.

In other words...in this passage, "I AM" is connected to "HEALER" and cannot be separated from it. Healing is not just what God does; it is WHO HE IS! For time and eternity.

He revealed HIMSELF as "JEHOVAH RAPHA."

And because Healer is who God is, sometimes God will bring you back to the bitter waters because He wants you to be healed, not because he is angry with you. He wants to remove your shame and give you peace. He desires to set you free from everything that will keep the journey from being an unhealthy journey.

That revelation was not just for the Jewish people. In Luke 4, Jesus stood in a synagogue one day, and the minister handed him a scroll that was Isaiah 61:

Jesus read it:

[18] "The Spirit of the Lord is upon me, for he has anointed me to bring Good News to the poor. He has sent me to proclaim that captives will be released, that the blind will see, that the oppressed will be set free, [19] and that the time of the Lord's favor has come." [20] He rolled up the scroll, handed it back to the attendant, and sat down. All eyes in the synagogue looked at him intently. [21] Then he began to speak to them. "The Scripture you've just heard has been fulfilled this very day!" (Luke 4:18-21, NLT)

In other words, the scripture that tied the power of God to your Messiah; your Healer, had just been revealed and fulfilled right in front of their eyes.

Jesus made a Qal to the very passage He was reading. He connected it as a current reality to Himself.

This fulfills Psalm 34:18, which says:

"The Lord is close to the broken hearted and saves those who are crushed in spirit." (NLT)

And again, in Psalm 147:3, "He heals the broken hearted and binds up their wounds." (NLT)

Healing that is not just physical, but potentially healing in every part of us. For the Jews, they needed healing from the parasites that infected their physical bodies, and we need healing from the things that affect our spirit. It must be said, however, that God is able to heal anything, whether it is spiritual, physically, emotional, or mental. He is HEALER.

Think about how important it is for God to reveal Himself to you as Healer.

All throughout the Bible, God reveals Himself as the God who heals. The Word is filled with references to healing, like this one from Psalm 103:3:

[3] He forgives all my sins and heals all my diseases. (NLT)

In the New Testament, Jesus is revealed as the one who heals in Matthew chapter 4:

[23] Jesus traveled throughout the region of Galilee, teaching in the synagogues and announcing the Good News about the Kingdom. And he healed every kind of disease and illness. [24] News about him spread as far as Syria, and people soon began bringing to him all who were sick. And whatever their sickness or disease, or if they were demon possessed or epileptic or paralyzed—he healed them all. (NLT)

And New Testament believers are called on to experience the revelation of God's healing power in their midst as well. It is not simply suggested, it is expected that God's people will do this, as He has revealed Himself as the God who heals. James writes,

¹³ Are any of you suffering hardships? You should pray. Are any of you happy? You should sing praises. ¹⁴ Are any of you sick? You should call for the elders of the church to come and pray over you, anointing you with oil in the name of the Lord. ¹⁵ Such a prayer offered in faith will heal the sick, and the Lord will make you well. And if you have committed any sins, you will be forgiven. ¹⁶ Confess your sins to each other and pray for each other so that you may be healed. The earnest prayer of a righteous person has great power and produces wonderful results. (James 5:13-16, NLT)

It's not enough to believe God can heal, but you must personally believe that He can heal *you!*

The revelation of God's healing power was also shown when Jesus was beaten before the crucifixion.

That's what Isaiah prophesied. ⁴ Yet it was our weaknesses he carried; it was our sorrows that weighed him down. And we thought his troubles were a punishment from God, a punishment for his own sins! ⁵ But he was pierced for our rebellion, crushed for our sins. He was beaten so we could be whole. He was whipped so we could be healed. (Isaiah 53:4-5, NLT)

He was revealed as the one who heals; He paid the price so we could be whole, He was whipped so we could be healed.

He wants you to be healed from the effects and diseases from your personal Egypt experience.

It was and is important for God reveal Himself to you in every way. That is not to say that God will heal us of every thing every time we come to a place of illness.

The goal is not just to heal, but also to reveal. God will use the bitter places to reveal His power and heal our diseases.

This alone should cause us to explode with gratitude that the creator of everything, the GOD who is all-powerful and all-knowing and holds everything together, loves us so much that He desires to lead us to places to reveal Himself to us, and in the process, reveal to us more about Himself than we could ever know.

Truly, He is an Amazing God!

This moment feels like an infomercial where we are amazed at the function of something, and the price has been revealed, making it a totally awesome experience, and then, the announcer says, "but wait, there's more!"

God does not just reveal Himself to us, or heal us, but God takes our weary bodies and tired spirits to a place just past the bitter place where He desires to refresh us. This is a vital next step. After cleansing comes refreshing.

It was after God revealed Himself as HEALER - the eternal HEALER - that he led them to a place to be refreshed with good, clear water to prepare them for the rest of the journey.

"After leaving Marah, the Israelites traveled on to the oasis of Elim, where they found twelve springs and seventy palm trees. They camped there beside the water." (Exodus 15:27,

NLT)

That's what the Holy Spirit does for us. Once we have been healed, or suffered the trial that has knocked us down, the Holy Spirit comes in and refreshes our lives so that we are ready for the rest of the journey. After cleansing, we need to be rehydrated.

Let Him do that for you now!

CHAPTER 6

THE PROVIDER

For thirty days, the Jews lived off of their provisions from Egypt. Now things were about to change.

"Then the whole community of Israel set out from Elim and journeyed into the wilderness of Sin, between Elim and Mount Sinai. They arrived there on the fifteenth day of the second month, one month after leaving the land of Egypt." (Exodus 16:1, NLT)

The journey that they were on was a spiritual journey of trust. Up until now, they had not had to trust God for food, only water to drink. But now, the food had run out and the people were getting hungry.

"There, too, the whole community of Israel complained about Moses and Aaron." (Exodus 16:2, NLT)

I don't know if the people understood that they would be trusting God the entire way, or if they started out having some preconceived notion that they would get to the Promised Land quickly. Instead, they became hungry with little means to provide their own food.

I have led or participated in seventeen teams overseas. On every trip, the trip itinerary is distributed to the travelers to help them feel a little more secure about their trip and to know what is planned next.

For the Jews, we don't get the idea that Moses' travel service provided them an itinerary for their trip. He just told them they were going to the Promised Land. The only notice they had for what was about to happen was real time. No advanced notice of impending events, or treasure maps holding the secret to a hidden cache of supplies for the journey.

This journey was God's idea, though. No one was fully prepared for the journey, and these steps proved it:

"If only the Lord had killed us back in Egypt," they moaned. "There we sat around pots filled with meat and ate all the bread we wanted. But now you have brought us into this wilderness to starve us all to death." (Exodus 16:3, NLT)

W. C. Kaiser notes, "This time the people "grumbled" (v.2) about the amount of food and the lack of meat (v.3). Suddenly Egypt seemed all peaches and cream (actually pots of meat and all you could eat—) rather than bondage and slave drivers. With a twisted piety and a condescending reference to Yahweh's name, the Israelites pretended that they would have preferred being victims at God's hand in Egypt to being the recipients of so many miracles—and all this hardship."[15]

Memory can be selective. The Jews did not sit around meat pots all day in Egypt. They didn't eat all the meat they wanted

---

[15] Kaiser, W. C., Jr. (1990). Exodus. In F. E. Gaebelein (Ed.), The Expositor's Bible Commentary: Genesis, Exodus, Leviticus, Numbers (Vol. 2, pp. 401–402). Grand Rapids, MI: Zondervan Publishing House.

and they did not have an abundance of bread. They were slaves, and at one time, they were forced to double their workload.

They were remembering a mirage. Mirages are those illusions where your eyes play tricks on you. In the desert you can see a mirage…a water hole, a watermelon…a Walmart. Just checking to see you if you are reading!

Our memories can do the same.

Sometimes we long for an illusion that we somehow remember to be true. We remember a time that time forgot. Somewhere in our past, we were set free from it and God did amazing things for us. He delivered us, but the longer we are away from that moment of deliverance, and hotter and dryer the desert, we tend to believe we had it better in Egypt. We believe it was somehow better before and we long to go back. Sometimes people try to go back. While the Jews did not, their longing for the 'good old days' hindered their trust of God.

Looking back can be bad for us, especially when it involves our life before Christ. There are at least three reasons it can be bad:

History without context is fantasy.

B. J. Neblett once wrote, "Fantasies… who needs fantasies? I have memories."

We can remember a good time in our past, but forget the other things that went along with it. We can remember living in a small apartment and say, those were good days, life was simpler then but we forget that the reason we were in the small apartment was because we were broke and had to eat ramen noodles for breakfast, lunch, and dinner. Also, we had to share our food with roaches and rats but those were the good old days.

The context behind the memory is important, but often the reason we miss the context is...

History without the whole story has holes in the story.

We forget the tough times, and remember the good times. We don't remember it all. Have you ever had a situation where you remembered the fun you had with a friend, and later in life, you reconnected and it didn't take long to remember why the friendship ended? Your history had holes in the story. We all have memory gaps...and only the strongest part of the memory lasts...but there are still holes in the story.

The Jews remembered stuff about Egypt, and their remembrance of their toil there was only about 30 days old. Even in that short of time, they forgot how things really were...and remembered a story that had holes in it.

Truly history is God's story; it is HIS STORY and His perspective of history is always best because ours is naturally skewed towards the fall (or sin) and not towards God and holiness.

I believe that is why Jesus was emphatic about looking back.

But Jesus told him, "Anyone who puts a hand to the plow and then looks back is not fit for the Kingdom of God." (Luke 9:62, NLT)

The Jews had a history with holes, but the third reason

looking back can be bad is

There is an odd comfort in the familiar

Our memories are selective but sometimes we find comfort in our pain. If we don't have that pain, the pain we are so used to, being pain free is hard to imagine. I have known people who were abused and they longed to go back to that time simply because it was the normal they knew. It was a horrible normal; it was a drama-filled normal; it was a painful normal but it was all they knew for so long.

What you call normal is not always good. NORMAL is what you are used to, not what is good or bad. I believe it is important that we stop looking back at what used to be our normal.

If you keep looking back, you are going to miss the Amazing things God is doing in front of you.

The most important thing they missed while they were longing for the 'good times in Egypt' was that God was doing AMAZING THINGS right in front of their eyes.

⁴"Then the Lord said to Moses, "Look, I'm going to rain down food from heaven for you. Each day the people can go out and pick up as much food as they need for that day. I will test them in this to see whether or not they will follow my instructions. ⁵ On the sixth day they will gather food, and when they prepare it, there will be twice as much as usual." (Exodus 16:4-5, NLT)

At this point, the Lord is establishing a touch point in their relationship with Him. If they obeyed and trusted God, they would be blessed. The blessing would be continual, not sporadic.

He had revealed Himself as deliverer, savior, healer, and now He would reveal Himself as their provider.

God's provision is always backed up by WHO HE IS…not WHAT HE DOES!

That never relieves us of our responsibility to obey.

God is going to bless you with money, not so you can buy a larger TV and pay off that one nagging bill, or get a cooler car, but He will bless you to see what you will do with that blessing.

Will you obey, or will you treat God's instruction with disdain?

"So Moses and Aaron said to all the people of Israel, "By evening you will realize it was the Lord who brought you out of the land of Egypt. ⁷ In the morning you will see the glory of the Lord, because he has heard your complaints, which are against him, not against us. What have we done that you should complain about us?" ⁸ Then Moses added, "The Lord will give you meat to eat in the evening and bread to satisfy you in the morning, for he has heard all your complaints against him. What have we done? Yes, your complaints are against the Lord, not against us." (Exodus 16:6-8, NLT)

God wanted to make the distinction that it was THE LORD who provided the bread and the meat, not Moses or

Aaron. That's important to remember. It was the LORD.

God wanted them to know that He was their provider.

It is imperative for you to realize that God is your source for everything. We think it is our employer. They are the one's that provide us a paycheck. We thank the employer because if it weren't for them, we wouldn't be able to pay our bills. In our thinking, our employer is the provider.

Or we think it is the government provide us a monthly check and EBT card, or Social Security. We wrongly think, "If it weren't for the government, I couldn't eat, wouldn't have a house, could not buy gas for my car. The government is my provider."

Or we think it is us, we invested wisely and due to our savvy investments, we now are blessed beyond measure; it was our doing. We think, "If it weren't for my wise investment strategy, I would have nothing. I have done well and provided for my family. I am my provider."

Ultimately, that is wrong.

The one that provides for you is the one who owns you!
Everything we have and everything we receive, is all because of God. He is the provider. We are not.

If we put ourselves or someone other than God in place as our provider, we are ascribing lordship of our finances to another entity. It owns us and in the most diabolical situations, you will compromise your beliefs to please an earthly provider.

In his book, *The Blessed Life*, Robert Morris writes about the "spirit of mammon." The spirit of mammon is a spirit that says that we don't need God, we are self-sufficient. We just need more money...not more of God. He shares a quote from Jimmy Evans, Pastor of Trinity Fellowship Church in Amarillo, Texas, which says, "Mammon promises us those things that only God can give—security, significance, identity, independence, power and freedom. Mammon tells us that it can insulate us from life's problems and that money is the answer to every situation." That thinking stands in direct opposition to the Word of God. Think about it, Mammon says buy and sell; God says to sow and reap. Mammon says to cheat and steal; God says to give and receive.

It is very important who you believe is your provider. If it is some entity other than God, you can trace the roots of that back to the spirit mammon and the spirit of mammon will not be satisfied until it has your soul.

"Jesus said this: [24] "No one can serve two masters. For you will hate one and love the other; you will be devoted to one and despise the other. You cannot serve both God and mammon. (Matthew 6:24, NLT)

Moses made the distinction that God is the source. It wasn't Moses; it wasn't Pharaoh, either. Because at this point, they were longing for a day when they got what they got because Pharaoh said they could have it.

Never long for your captor's provision when you can eat provisions from the KING of the AGES.

"Then Moses said to Aaron, "Announce this to the entire community of Israel: 'Present yourselves before the Lord, for he has heard your complaining.' " 10 And as Aaron spoke to the whole community of Israel, they looked out toward the wilderness." (Exodus 16:9-10, NLT)

For a minute, they stopped looking back and looked toward the wilderness. This is key because of what was in the wilderness, there they could see the awesome glory of the Lord in the cloud.

I have seen it over and over in my life. I can tell you story after story of God providing in miraculous ways for missions trips, personal finances, church finances, you name it. God moved powerfully so many times. God moved in powerful ways…and made a way when there was no way.

If you always look back, you will miss what God is doing right in front of you right now!

God is moving in your life right now. IN YOUR LIFE! You may not know it, but if you will look closely at your life, there is a place where God is moving in your life. I want you to say it out loud: GOD IS DOING SOMETHING IN MY LIFE.

Stop looking back, and look to the LORD.

If you are not seeing it, you are letting the enemy cloud your perspective, or you are looking the wrong way, at the wrong thing. God is AMAZING! He has a way of displaying His power all around for the Jews in that moment, they stopped looking back at Pharaoh and started looking toward the wilderness. It was there that they could see the awesome glory of the Lord in the cloud.

[11]"Then the Lord said to Moses, [12]"I have heard the

Israelites' complaints. Now tell them, 'In the evening you will have meat to eat, and in the morning you will have all the bread you want. Then you will know that I am the Lord your God.' " (Exodus 16:11-12, NLT)

Get ready, you are about to be blessed. You will have meat, you will have bread. ALL YOU WANT!!!!!! This stands in stark contrast to Egypt where they did not sit around pots of meat and all you can eat bread buffets. They were hungry in Egypt.

But wait, they were in the desert. There was no meat anywhere around them. There was no flour, no wheat, nothing that can indicate that they were going to have anything miraculous, except for the word of the LORD.

Would that be enough for you? Would God's word be enough for you? Do you need to see something, in order to believe something?

Do you need to see the seed before you see the harvest? Do you need assurance that God will not let you down?

If so, you can measure your growth in God by reading His word and believing Him without seeing anything. You can see how your trust in God has grown by how much you believe without having to see. Especially in the storm. If you can believe God in the midst of the worst storm, or the problem that is staring you down you can keep from doubting and continue to believe then you are making progress. If you can stare down your storm without blinking, you have arrived.

Well, maybe not arrived, but you certainly are on the right road.

That is what God is doing now: He is measuring the Jews to see if they will believe.

This may be the point that you say, LORD I BELIEVE, BUT HELP MY UNBELIEF. Especially if you are struggling with trusting God to do what He said He would do.

Stepping out in faith is trust when God says to do it, but foolishness if we do it without God.

The Jews were then served up a lesson on provision and the goodness of God:

"That evening vast numbers of quail flew in and covered the camp. And the next morning the area around the camp was wet with dew. [14] When the dew evaporated, a flaky substance as fine as frost blanketed the ground. [15] The Israelites were puzzled when they saw it. "What is it?" they asked each other. They had no idea what it was. And Moses told them, "It is the food the Lord has given you to eat. [16] These are the Lord's instructions: Each household should gather as much as it needs. Pick up two quarts for each person in your tent." [17] So the people of Israel did as they were told. Some gathered a lot, some only a little. [18] But when they measured it out, everyone had just enough. Those who gathered a lot had nothing left over, and those who gathered only a little had enough. Each family had just what it needed." (Exodus 16:13-18, NLT)

God gave them quail in the evening. So much meat that it

covered the camp. Their dinner was quail and the next morning God would provide them.

The bread God provided was unlike anything they had ever seen. It was bread in the desert. They were to pick it up and eat it that day.

"Then Moses told them, "Do not keep any of it until morning." [20] But some of them didn't listen and kept some of it until morning. But by then it was full of maggots and had a terrible smell. Moses was very angry with them. (Exodus 16:19-20, NLT)

How did Moses know about this? Probably because they were complaining about the smell and the maggots.

"After this the people gathered the food morning by morning, each family according to its need. And as the sun became hot, the flakes they had not picked up melted and disappeared. [22] On the sixth day, they gathered twice as much as usual—four quarts for each person instead of two. Then all the leaders of the community came and asked Moses for an explanation. [23] He told them, "This is what the Lord commanded: Tomorrow will be a day of complete rest, a holy Sabbath day set apart for the Lord. So bake or boil as much as you want today, and set aside what is left for tomorrow." [24] So they put some aside until morning, just as Moses had commanded. And in the morning the leftover food was wholesome and good, without maggots or odor. [25] Moses said, "Eat this food today, for today is a Sabbath day dedicated to the Lord. There will be no food on the ground today. [26] You may gather the food for six days, but the seventh day is the Sabbath. There will be no food on the ground that day."

²⁷ Some of the people went out anyway on the seventh day, but they found no food. ²⁸ The Lord asked Moses, "How long will these people refuse to obey my commands and instructions? ²⁹ They must realize that the Sabbath is the Lord's gift to you. That is why he gives you a two-day supply on the sixth day, so there will be enough for two days. On the Sabbath day you must each stay in your place. Do not go out to pick up food on the seventh day." ³⁰ So the people did not gather any food on the seventh day. ³¹ The Israelites called the food manna. It was white like coriander seed, and it tasted like honey wafers. "(Exodus 16:21-31, NLT)

The people struggled with obedience. The instructions were clear. But some kept the bread until the next day. It stunk and had maggots. God gave them bread, every day of the week, except on the sixth day, when they would have gathered enough for the seventh day too. This continued for the entire time they were in the wilderness. FORTY YEARS!!!!!!

When I say that God has your back, it is true. If He leads you to the desert, He is "all in" for the journey. In fact, whatever journey you are on, whatever storm you are facing, whatever struggle you feel, whatever you are going through, if God brought you to this point, He will not leave you, He will not abandon you. He is "all in."

If you went into the desert without God's direction, and you are on your own, then you need for God to redeem the moment you are in, and allow Him control of your future. You need Him to rescue you; call on God to come to your aid, and He will help you.

But if God brought you to the desert, then it is up to Him to provide for you. It's not up to you. It's not up to me. It is up to God. He will do this to reveal HIMSELF to you as your provider.

One day, Jesus fed thousands with a few loaves of bread and fish. This miracle blew people away. From that feeding of the five thousand, the disciples set out for Capernaum and during the night, Jesus walked on the water. It was a powerful time for everyone. The people that Jesus fed the day before could not find Jesus the next day so they found out that the disciples went across the Sea of Galilee, and that Jesus did too, so they set out to find Jesus.

When they found Jesus, He said, you only seek me because you are hungry, not because you want to understand what the miracles mean. Jesus told them that they should do the work of God...and the greatest work of God is to believe in the one GOD SENT. In other words, to believe in JESUS.

"They answered, "Show us a miraculous sign if you want us to believe in you. What can you do? [31] After all, our ancestors ate manna while they journeyed through the wilderness! The Scriptures say, 'Moses gave them bread from heaven to eat.'" (John 6:30-31, NLT)

Did Moses give them bread in the wilderness? NO!

God did!!!!

Check this out: God doesn't waste a miracle, and that story with Moses and the Jews was all for a purpose and hundreds and hundreds of years later, God designed that story to give the Jews Manna to feed them, but also to point to someone greater than the bread in the wilderness! Now look at the next verse in John 6:

"Jesus said, "I tell you the truth, Moses didn't give you bread from heaven. My Father did. And now he offers you the true bread from heaven. [33] The true bread of God is the one who comes down from heaven and gives life to the world." [34] "Sir," they said, "give us that bread every day." (John 6:32-34, NLT)

How many would say, "I want THAT kind of bread?"

"Jesus replied, "I am the bread of life. Whoever comes to me will never be hungry again. Whoever believes in me will never be thirsty. [36] But you haven't believed in me even though you have seen me. [37] However, those the Father has given me will come to me, and I will never reject them. [38] For I have come down from heaven to do the will of God who sent me, not to do my own will. [39] And this is the will of God, that I should not lose even one of all those he has given me, but that I should raise them up at the last day. [40] For it is my Father's will that all who see his Son and believe in him should have eternal life. I will raise them up at the last day." [41] Then the people began to murmur in disagreement because he had said, "I am the bread that came down from heaven." [42] They said, "Isn't this Jesus, the son of Joseph? We know his father and mother. How can he say, 'I came down from heaven'?" (John 6:35-42, NLT)

You have got to see this: In the Old Testament story, the Jews looked at the manna in the wilderness and said, "what is it?" They looked at the bread and asked…what is it?

So, in this story in John 6, Jesus tells them, I am the bread that came down from heaven. The people of Jesus' day looked at Jesus and said, "Who is it?"

"But Jesus replied, "Stop complaining about what I said. ⁴⁴ For no one can come to me unless the Father who sent me draws them to me, and at the last day I will raise them up… ⁴⁸ Yes, I am the bread of life! ⁴⁹ Your ancestors ate manna in the wilderness, but they all died. ⁵⁰ Anyone who eats the bread from heaven, however, will never die. (John 6:43-50, NLT)

Jesus is the manna everyone is looking for: a bread that brings life. The manna in the wilderness is gone, so is Egypt. They are all in the past, now God is about to show them something AMAZING, that His son is the true bread from heaven.

God gave manna in the wilderness to feed people, not only to teach them to trust and obey His word, but to ultimately point to something greater: the true bread that comes to give life to every man.

It is important to recognize something today. GOD IS GOOD. He loves you and has your best interest at heart. He will shut some doors, allow some doors to open and even step out of the way if you are stubborn and demand to do your own thing.

We always want God to intervene and keep us from a storm,

but rarely do we want to obey and trust Him so we don't get into the storm. God wanted the Jews to know He was their provider, and literally was providing for them every single day. He loved them. He wanted the best for them. He was going to move in their lives in greater ways than they had ever experienced, but they had to trust Him.

I don't know if they ever thought that God was good or that the bread He gave every day was always there and God could be trusted to bring about good things, or if they just expected it without being thankful. I don't know their heart, but I do know mine.

I can be selfish, unthankful, and can miss what God is doing when I complain about what is going on instead of seeing that God is doing AMAZING THINGS all around me. I can become focused on the wrong things, and miss the good things. I can even miss the fact that God is my provider and begin to believe that I have what I have and I get what I get because of my efforts or someone else's provision.

Today, that has to end. I want to enjoy the blessings of God, giving Him full glory for providing for me.

If you want to enjoy the goodness of God, you have to stop looking at others to provide for you, and start looking to God to provide. Stop hoping something will come your way as a blessing from a man, or a company, or yourself and look to God. You may work for a company, or have some type of government check, but today, you should say, "God thank you for providing for my needs, YOU ARE MY PROVIDER!"

And He has enough to supply your needs: "And this same God who takes care of me will supply all your needs from his glorious riches, which have been given to us in Christ Jesus." (Philippians 4:19, NLT)

All of your needs are taken care of because of Jesus Christ. From salvation, to your daily bread, God is your provider. Recognize that today, and prepare to experience the provision of an AMAZING GOD!

CHAPTER 7

FOR THOSE WHO ARE THIRSTY

Have you ever witnessed a water dowser trying to find water? A water dowser is someone who uses some type of wood, rod, or pendulum to find water under the soil's surface. He or she walks around with the implement and at the moment the water is found, the wood, rod, or pendulum points down. This method has been used for thousands of years and is a controversial method for locating water under the ground surface. Hydrologists tend to prefer a more scientific method of locating water, yet the dowsing community continues to use this ancient method. There is even a governing body that oversees and governs the activities of 'dowsers.' [16]

Regardless of the method you use, water is essential to life, and in the desert, thirst can quickly lead to death. It is vital that no time is wasted in search of water. After finding water at Marah, the people moved from there to Elim, and then God led them from that place to another stop on the journey.

At the LORD's command, the whole community of Israel left the wilderness of Sin and moved from place to place. Eventually they camped at Rephidim, but there was no water there for the people to drink. (Exodus 16:1, NLT)

It would seem strange to camp at Rephidim if there was no

---

[16] http://dowsers.org/

water, but there was a reason the people stopped. In this area, there is something known as a "wadi." A wadi is a dry riverbed in a valley, where water is known to flow. Sometimes, just a little digging in the wadi will reveal a water source. In the desert, it is very easy to see where water is, or has been...so the people must have camped there anticipating that water would flow in the wadi.

Unfortunately, there was no water for the people to drink. At the very place that water should have been, there was none. It was like a mirage.

Sometimes what looks like a nice place turns dry and desolate quickly. The refreshing place is only a mirage and we are left to wonder why the 'supposed refreshing' place is so dry.

It is important to remember that the Jews had traveled to Rephidim specifically "as the Lord commanded." In his wisdom, God had directed his people to move from the Desert of Sin (where they hungered but afterwards were satisfied) to Rephidim (where they thirsted).

Let's establish something that is imperative for anyone on the journey with God. This was God's doing. One cannot appreciate power until they are weak, one cannot appreciate healing unless one is sick. One cannot appreciate food unless one is hungry, and one cannot fully appreciate water unless they are extremely thirsty.

God may take you somewhere to appreciate where you have been...or appreciate where you are...or to experience His power over your circumstances.

God may have brought you to a place where you can

empathize with someone going through something because you have been there. You know exactly what it feels like to be homeless, broke, poor, in pain, hungry, thirsty, or in great need because of your experience, and one day, another traveler will want to know how to make it. Sometimes God leads you on the path of barrenness to help those who have a life worse than yours find their way to God.

Even though God was the one leading the people, they still struggled with where He had led them.

[2] So once more the people complained against Moses. "Give us water to drink!" they demanded. (Exodus 16:2, NLT)

The phrase, "Give us water to drink!" was a demand based on what God did through the quail and manna in the Desert of Sin, and was like someone saying, "Do a magic trick for us like you did last time."

In other words, they treated God's provision as a fluke or a deceptive trick that worked to feed them, and they wanted the same for water.

We have to be careful that we don't look at God's provision as a fluke. The provision of manna was not about what God did, it was about WHO HE WAS: THE PROVIDER. The people were looking at God satisfying their thirst the same way...as a fluke, or worse...a magic trick. God never desires to prove anything, nor is He desiring to show you something that will cause you to be amazed by what He can do. But He does want you to know WHO HE IS...

"Moses then said: "Quiet!" "Why are you complaining against me? And why are you testing the LORD?" (Exodus 16:3,

NLT)

Instead of submitting to the *tests* God was conducting for them, Israel began to *test* the Lord. This 'testing' the Lord was not a good thing and the generations that would later come were reminded of the failing philosophy of testing the Lord;

"Yet how quickly they forgot what he had done!
    They wouldn't wait for his counsel!
14 In the wilderness their desires ran wild,
    testing God's patience in that dry wasteland. (Psalms 106:13-14, NLT)

God's people tempt or test the Lord when they distrust His kindness and providential care of them and grumble against Him and/or His leaders.

Moses would later warn (Deuteronomy 6:16) that men were not to put God to the test as they did at Massah.

3 But tormented by thirst, they continued to argue with Moses. "Why did you bring us out of Egypt? Are you trying to kill us, our children, and our livestock with thirst?" (Exodus 17:3, NLT)

When a person is tormented by thirst, they find a powerful moment when the body is screaming for water and there is none to find. I don't know if you have ever been there or not, but you probably have been in some desperate situation where panic was close at hand.

It is that one moment of desperation when every cell in your body is crying out for something.

It may be love...you are wounded and you just need

someone to love you.

It may be comfort...you are hurting and just need someone to hold you.

It may be extreme fear and panic...and you need someone to bring you peace, right now.

It may be that you are dry emotionally... and you need someone to quench that thirst for joy, or peace, or sanity.

Sometimes the desperation is different. It is the trouble that stays on our mind that won't let go.

It's the feeling you have nothing left, even finding yourself looking through the couch cushions for change to put gas in the car.

Sometimes God leads us to desperation to show us His all-surpassing power. Sometimes God leads us to desperation to show us our character.

⁴ Then Moses cried out to the LORD, "What should I do with these people? They are ready to stone me!" (Exodus 16:4, NLT)

Moses did the right thing. He took his problem to the Lord in prayer. We do well to spend our energy taking our need to God in prayer rather than to social media, our friends, or to anyone that we may think might help us. Go to God FIRST!!!!!

Then do what He tells you to do. Be obedient. God will use your hunger, your fear, your worry, and take you to the edge of your ability and your want, calling you to draw closer to HIM. He is trying to teach you to trust Him, and to rely on Him. He wants you to learn to depend on Him and He will keep bringing you to Rephidim (to the place of your thirst), or to the desert place (the place of your hunger) to teach you trust.

⁵ The LORD said to Moses, "Walk out in front of the people. Take your staff, the one you used when you struck the water of the Nile, and call some of the elders of Israel to join you."(Exodus 16:5, NLT)

Notice this was not done in the shadows. God told Moses to walk out in front of the people. He told him to bring the elders.

God was going to demonstrate something powerful to the people. But it was more than just displaying God's ability to bring water from an unlikely source. God brings us to these times to demonstrate more than what He can *do*, but He does it because He wants us to know *who He is*. He does it because He loves us and sometimes the only way for you to even turn to Him is for you to get desperate.

The next verse says:

⁶ I will stand before you on the rock at Mount Sinai. Strike the rock, and water will come gushing out. Then the people will be able to drink." So Moses struck the rock as he was told, and water gushed out as the elders looked on. (Exodus 16:6, NLT)

This water source came from a rock, and with one strike from a staff, enough water flowed for about four million people.

One strike and an abundant supply of water flowed.

The people were so close to the source but did not know

it, and allowed desperation to win the day.

We get desperate, too. Sometimes we get desperate because we bring desperate things on ourselves. I know I have. I have made senseless choices that brought me to desperation and a call for God to bail me out. I know I am not alone in this.

But, it is important to know that sometimes God leads us to desperate places too. Just because you are following God's will does not mean that there may not be moments were you feel desperate.

Webster's Dictionary defines the word, "desperate" this way: "feeling, showing, or involving a hopeless sense that a situation is so bad as to be impossible to deal with."

When God leads you to a desperate place, that place is not to take your hope, but to cause you to see what God is doing. That desperate place is just the location where it is vital that you look for the activity of God around you. Wherever the activity of God is greatest, then the miracle is within striking distance.

The answer is as close as a staff striking a rock.

The Jews were complaining about leadership, and even looking for rocks to throw at Moses when the answer to their desperation was a rock three feet away from Moses.

We get so close to the miracle, and then doubt pushes us away. We get so close to the answer, but we let fear blind us from seeing it. We get so desperate that we fail to see the activity of God and the answer to our prayer. God was there. They just couldn't connect God's presence to their great need.

This is the truth: He is always THAT CLOSE.

And He answered their prayer.

⁷ Moses named the place Massah (which means "test") and Meribah (which means "arguing") because the people of Israel argued with Moses and tested the LORD by saying, "Is the LORD here with us or not?"(Exodus 17:7, NLT)

Kaiser wrote, "In less than six months they had witnessed ten plagues, pillars of cloud and fire, the opening and shutting of the Red Sea, the miraculous sweetening of the water, and the sending of food and meat from heaven; yet their real question came down to this: 'Is the LORD among us or not?'"[17]

Is the Lord here with us or not? That is the question that sounds like a taunt from the devil. "Is the Lord really here?" is a question that rings in our ears and flows from our mouths, just like the Jews. We ask:

Does the Lord really care?

Does the Lord really love me?

Can the Lord really do anything about this situation?

All the while, there is this nagging taunt that emboldens such thinking in our mind. It becomes a haunting taunt from the enemy that can destroy our hope and debilitate our faith.

Often, like the Jews, we continue to take the bait of the taunt and question God:

In Psalms 78, scripture reveals a sad commentary:

---

[17] Kaiser, W. C., Jr. (1990). Exodus. In F. E. Gaebelein (Ed.), *The Expositor's Bible Commentary: Genesis, Exodus, Leviticus, Numbers* (Vol. 2, pp. 406–407). Grand Rapids, MI: Zondervan Publishing House.

[56] But they kept testing and rebelling against God Most High. They did not obey his laws. (NLT)

Later in the journey to the Promised Land, there was another time when the people were thirsty and needed water from a rock. That event is found in Numbers 20:1–13. It is at the end of the 40 years of wandering in the desert. In this account, the glory of the Lord is not present; and Moses is explicitly instructed that he is not to strike the rock but only to speak to it.

Instead, he asks the people if he and Aaron were supposed to get water for them and in that moment instead of speaking to the rock, Moses strikes it.

God was very angry because He was trying to use to reveal Himself to the people in greater measure. Instead, Moses used this powerful moment as his own, revealing nothing but arrogance and pride.

Both of these desperate situations were moments the people could have learned to trust God. Even better, they could have allowed these moments to deepen their walk with God, and come to know Him in greater measure.

That was always the goal, but during the lifetime of the people, it was something they never understood. They treated God like some people treat a rich uncle: they never really knew him, only used him to get what they could.

While the people missed it, God did not waste this moment.

In fact, God set up these 'thirsty' events as an annual time of remembering the wandering in the desert. The event was called the Feast of Tabernacles and the people would stay in a sukkah, which was a temporary structure, like their ancestors stayed in the desert, during the celebration.

They would eat, celebrate, and remember what God did for their ancestors in the wilderness. It was meant to point people to God.

At the Feast of Tabernacles, the people would celebrate for eight days. It was required that every man appear before the Lord at the sanctuary during this festival.

At the time of the morning sacrifice, the people took branches of palm, myrtle, and willow and marched around the altar of burnt offering once daily and seven times on the 7th day which commemorated the victory at Jericho.

On the eighth and final day, they would commemorate their thirst and God's provision in the desert.

This was the culmination of the feast and it was the most solemn and community-oriented time of the week.

On the eight day, a priest would fill a golden vessel with water from the pool of Siloam- this flowed from Hezekiah's fountain.

While he dipped the vessel into the water the people would repeatedly quote Isaiah 55:1, "Come, all you who are thirsty, come to the waters; and you who have no money, come, buy and eat". As they repeated in unison, the scripture sounded like a chant as the people quoted this powerful verse over and over in anticipation of the events that followed.

As the priest made his way back to the temple area, with the water-filled vessel, the people continued the chant, and on arriving to the temple area, he was greeted with a trumpet blast and then, someone would sound out the words of Isaiah 12:3: "with joy you will draw water from the wells of salvation"

At this moment, the priest would raise his left hand to quiet the people, and with his right hand, would raise up the vessel to pour out the water next to the altar of burnt offerings. The people would become as silent and still as possible so they could hear the water being poured out.

It is at this very moment, as the people were silent, and the priest was about to pour the water from the vessel that this story unfolds:

John 7:37-39: [37] On the last and greatest day of the Feast, Jesus stood and said in a loud voice, "If anyone is thirsty, let him come to me and drink. [38] Whoever believes in me, as the Scripture has said, streams of living water will flow from within him." [39] By this he meant the Spirit, whom those who believed in him were later to receive. Up to that time the Spirit had not been given, since Jesus had not yet been glorified. (NIV)

Everything they looked for in the desert was found in Christ. At this one moment, as the vessel was about to be emptied and the people would remember their thirst, Jesus let them know that He was truly what they were searching for...not water from A ROCK...but water from THE ROCK!

That is God's same desire for you and me. He wants you to find your thirst quenched by His presence. Not by some type of watering hole of our making, or even a refreshing place that someone else has made; God desires that we find in Him all that we long for.

Be assured that God has provided us all that we need. He desires to live in us and work through us. What Jesus was describing was the Baptism in the Holy Spirit! It is the water he was describing.

John 7:38-39 reads, [38]"Whoever believes in me, as the Scripture has said, streams of living water will flow from within him." [39] By this he meant the Spirit, whom those who believed in him were later to receive. Up to that time the Spirit had not been given, since Jesus had not yet been glorified. (NIV)

The 'streams of living water' that flow from Christ are always satisfying, refreshing, and life-giving. Our desperation should always drive us to Him!

We live our lives as desperate people. Desperate for love, affection, peace, joy, life. We are desperate for food, water, and a lot of things that bring us problems. For all that we are hungry for, and for the desperate thirst we have, God wants us to see Him as the source of provision for every dry and empty place we come to in our lives. He wants to reveal Himself as an Amazing God that satisfies all of the longings we all have. What the Jews did not understand, and what we should get powerfully, is that God wants us to know Him the same way: as the One who satisfies the longing in our lives.

That's God's heart for you and me; it is why Jesus came to earth. It is why the Holy Spirit was poured out on the Day of Pentecost and just like the Jews found with Moses, the answer to your longing is always within striking distance.

CHAPTER 8

———————◆◆———————

AMAZING WARRIOR

One would think that the Jews would be in awe of God's power. Until now, God proved greater than Egypt's gods, He delivered the people from their bondage, healed them, provided food, and even made water flow from a rock. For anyone gazing on such a sight from a distance, it should cause immense fear. Instead, it provided the right ingredients for jealousy and hostility to grow with those in the desert.

I believe that when there is great activity of God in your life, the enemy will do everything he can to pick a fight to distract you from the journey God has you on. In fact, you can rest assured that there will be someone that will gripe and complain about what you are doing, question your motives, talk about you behind your back and try to make God's blessings a curse on you.

It's not always the most evil people. Sometimes its people who know God, or should know better. A case in point is found in Exodus 17: ⁸ While the people of Israel were still at Rephidim, the warriors of Amalek attacked them. (NLT)

The Jews were at the very place God provided water from a rock and the warriors of Amalek attacked them at this place. This is significant because they had found gold in the desert: Water. It was not just a little water. It was enough to give water for a long period of time to hundreds of thousands of people. Such a blessing cannot go unpunished.

These were not just any warriors. The people of Amalek were descendants of Esau. Remember Esau? He was the one who sold his birthright for a bowl of stew. He lost the blessing from his dad Isaac, instead the blessing went to Jacob, whose name was changed to (wait for it, wait for it)...Israel.

I am sure that the descendants of Esau knew the whole story, so there was no love lost on the descendants of Jacob. Hard feelings don't pass away with a passing generation, so it begs the question: was it hatred from the people of Amalek due to their family history or jealousy over water rights that drove them to fight the Jews?

If it was hatred, they were missing out on the blessing. They could have blessed God's chosen people. Don't ever set yourself up to hate anyone, especially a child of God.

It is so important that if you have been offended, go to that person and get it settled: forgiven and under the blood of Jesus.

Never let your offenses make Satan famous, instead, let reconciliation and forgiveness bring glory to God!

Hatred may have caused the problem between the Amalekites and the Jews, but it also could have been jealousy over water rights. Not everyone enjoys seeing others prosper.

Jealousy is the banner of insecurity!
A jealous spirit is also a fighting spirit, fighting those who have

what they want. The fight is not direct, but instead will focus on the character of the man or woman, attempts to disgrace the family, tearing down the job, disparaging the marriage or question the prosperity's origin; not because they want it, but because they can't have it. They will denigrate anyone who does.

The people of Amalek were descendants of Abraham, just like the Jews. They knew the promises given to Abraham and to his seed. They were his descendants, but could not claim the promises because they failed the believing and obeying test, that's why they were stuck in the desert and not enjoying Canaan.

Don't be surprised if you are attacked by people that claim to be believers. Don't be amazed that people will be jealous about the good things God is doing in your life, even others who claim Christ. You will probably find yourself in the middle of a battle because of it.

Exodus 17 states, [9] Moses commanded Joshua, "Choose some men to go out and fight the army of Amalek for us. Tomorrow, I will stand at the top of the hill, holding the staff of God in my hand." (NLT)

To direct the battle against the Amalekites, Moses called a young man from the tribe of Ephraim (Joseph's son) named Joshua, by this time, Joshua was the young age of 45.

Joshua was to muster an army to fight against the Amalekites while Moses, with the staff of God in his hand, stood on top of one of the nearby hills overlooking the plain.

Two elements were to be operating, the sword in Joshua's

hand and the staff (symbol of divine intervention) in Moses' hand.

I like what W.C. Kaiser wrote: Once again divine sovereignty and human responsibility were linked in carrying out the will of God.[18]

That is a spiritual principle we touched on in a previous chapter. The Jews wanted magic when it came to water for their thirst. They wanted to watch, and not have any responsibility.

Instead this principle shows up in virtually every miracle in the Old and New Testament. God does His part, and we do our part. His divine sovereignty and our responsibility are linked to carry out God's will and to see a miracle happen.

So, check this out. God may tell you that He is going to bless you and then He will call you to give all your savings to Him. Or, He will tell you that a miracle is coming your way, you just have to do one thing.

It is a Biblical principle for miracles found in both Old and New Testament:

In the Old Testament, a man named Namaan, had to dip in the muddy Jordan River seven times. In the New Testament, the man born blind had to wash his eyes in the pool. The boy with the bread and fish had to give up his lunch

---

[18] Kaiser, W. C., Jr. (1990). Exodus. In F. E. Gaebelein (Ed.), *The Expositor's Bible Commentary: Genesis, Exodus, Leviticus, Numbers* (Vol. 2, p. 408). Grand Rapids, MI: Zondervan Publishing House.

for the miracle to come. The lame man had to stand up. Think about that a minute, the lame man in Acts 3 is sitting lame (unable to walk). It is apparent he cannot walk but what command did Peter and John give him? Stand up and walk.

Sounds kind of dumb, right? But it was the test of faith. I don't know if he felt something or not or if he simply obeyed, but for whatever reason, he leapt to his feet and starting skipping.

Our miracle will be a similar test of faith, one that will challenge you to do the incredible or give the impossible. Once you do your small part, God will do His amazing part. Then, you will experience a biblical miracle.

God can do the miracle without your help, but he wants you to have a part in the process. Without your commitment, the miracle will lose its power because you will begin to view it as magic, natural phenomenon, or just one of those things.

The story in Exodus 17 continues:[10] So Joshua did what Moses had commanded and fought the army of Amalek. Meanwhile, Moses, Aaron, and Hur climbed to the top of a nearby hill.

In the valley, was the battle where Joshua and his warriors fought the army of Amalek. Moses, Aaron and Hur climbed to the top of a hill to do their part.

Not everyone has the same gifts, but everyone has a part to play in the battle.

[11] As long as Moses held up the staff in his hand, the Israelites had the advantage. But whenever he dropped his

hand, the Amalekites gained the advantage. (Exodus 17:11, NLT)

Now, this is a great picture...."as long as" Moses held up his hands (presumably with staff alternately in one or the other), Joshua and his men were victorious. However, "whenever he lowered his hands" through weariness, the Amalekites forged ahead in the battle.

The gesture of raising the hands was not just to encourage those in the battle. It wasn't that moment when the warriors, weary from battle would look to their leader on the hill and in dramatic fashion, would summon the inner courage to fight with greater intensity.

It wasn't the encouragement that would win the battle.

The gesture of raising the hands was not just to pray. It wasn't just an outward sign of something with empty form, such as those who get in the prayer position but not really praying but instead, are just posing as a person of prayer.

The gesture of raising the hands and a staff symbolized Moses's appeal to God. But it was no magic wand. It was a prophetic action of the upraised hands that signaled the fervent prayers of the heart of Moses as he witnessed the battle, and the activity of God moving when Moses was obedient.

The same is true for you and me. Coupled with obedience, fervent prayers have great power for the child of God.

Then, the story takes a turn: [12] Moses' arms soon became so tired he could no longer hold them up. So Aaron and Hur found a stone for him to sit on. Then they stood on each side of Moses, holding up his hands. So his hands held steady until sunset.

Even though Moses was obedient, he became weary. He needed his brothers to come alongside and help him. They could not win unless they helped hold their brother's hands up until the battle was finished.

This should be a great template for life. You are not an island. Sometimes, even in your obedience, you will grow weary. When you grow weary, and you are alone, you are the most vulnerable. If you have been doing your very best to follow God and the battle's have been intense, you have probably found yourself suffering set-backs and struggles. Unfortunately, the battle does not stop because you are tired.

That is why finding a strong, Bible-believing church is crucial to continued victories in your life. If you are surrounded by people that understand the need to help you in your fight against the enemy, and they willingly step up to fight alongside you, then you will find great victory. Alone, you are vulnerable, but with a contingent of believers, you are positioned for greatness.

It is important to note that even the best warriors get weary. You may feel that you have shared your struggles with enough people, that they are weary of hearing about it. You might even hear the enemy taunt you to keep it to yourself. You feel that no one cares, or that even if they did know your struggles, they would not be able to do anything about it. All the while, Satan desires to sift you as wheat.

You might even want your struggles to remain your struggles, fearing that if people really knew you, that they would not like you. So, you put on your 'Sunday morning mask' to cover up your battles and baggage.

Never let "fake it till you make it" become your mantra!

All the while, Satan is laughing his head off because of your pride.

It is pride to think you can make it through this life alone. If you try, you will be defeated quickly.

You are most vulnerable when you are isolated away from your support.

The picture of these men holding up the arms of Moses is not just a great picture for people to come alongside the pastor and hold his hands up so that the battle can be won, but for every believer to do that for others, so it can be done for you.

I am a firm believer that if you are struggling and feel alone, find someone and hold their arms up, encourage them, pray for them, believe with them, stand up for them and help them.

If you are waiting for someone to do that for you, why not start the ball rolling yourself? Why not be the one who does it, who steps out and lifts up someone else's arm? You will find that lifting others, lifts your spirit. The longer you are focused on your own life, the quicker you lose the battle.

It's time to get a breakthrough so that you can help others get a breakthrough. I know I keep poking the bear with this point. Here is a word from God for you. Stop the "Lone Ranger" thinking. Even the "LONE" Ranger had Tonto.

Stop doing this thing alone. Start looking around you for people who are in the battle and lift up their arms.

I like what the Apostle Paul wrote. He had just talked about Jesus coming quickly in the rapture and then he writes:

4 But you aren't in the dark about these things, dear brothers and sisters, and you won't be surprised when the day of the Lord comes like a thief. 5 For you are all children of the light and of the day; we don't belong to darkness and night. 6 So be on your guard, not asleep like the others. Stay alert and be clearheaded. 7 Night is the time when people sleep and drinkers get drunk. 8 But let us who live in the light be clearheaded, protected by the armor of faith and love, and wearing as our helmet the confidence of our salvation. 9 For God chose to save us through our Lord Jesus Christ, not to pour out his anger on us. 10 Christ died for us so that, whether we are dead or alive when he returns, we can live with him forever. 11 So encourage each other and build each other up, just as you are already doing. (1 Thessalonians 5:4-11, NLT)

At the moment Jesus was pressed by circumstances and was about to be arrested, the moment where He had to ask the Father to let the cup pass from Him, he wanted his brothers with him praying. He wanted them there to hold up his hands for the greatest battle anyone has ever faced ever.

They could not pray one hour. We have to do better. Look around your life, right now. Look for people you can lift with your words, and with your prayers.

When we do, we experience victory, and they experience victory. As we find in the story of Moses.

[13] As a result, Joshua overwhelmed the army of Amalek in battle.

Finally the lengthy battle came to an end, with Joshua as victor.[19]

The battle was not his alone. People lifted Moses' arms, Moses was committed to holding up his arms, and the Lord showed His amazing power; each of these elements brought about the victory.

Could God have taken care of the enemy all by Himself? Of course, but He chose to use His power, through His people to win the victory.

He is still doing that today. He is using your battle, and your battle partner to win the victory...don't try to go it alone.

[14] After the victory, the LORD instructed Moses, "Write this down on a scroll as a permanent reminder, and read it aloud to Joshua: I will erase the memory of Amalek from under heaven."

[15] Moses built an altar there and named it Yahweh-nissi (which means "the LORD is my banner").

The Lord is my banner. Review this story for a moment: Moses is on a hill, hands lifted high, while an intense battle is being fought in the valley. As long as Moses hands are lifted, the war plan was successful. When they were not, then the battle suffered.

---

[19] Kaiser, W. C., Jr. (1990). Exodus. In F. E. Gaebelein (Ed.), *The Expositor's Bible Commentary: Genesis, Exodus, Leviticus, Numbers* (Vol. 2, pp. 408–409). Grand Rapids, MI: Zondervan Publishing House.

In this context, the word, "banner" (*nēs*) reflects the root "to be high," "raised," or "conspicuous." The allusion would be to lifting up the staff as a standard and a testimony to his power.[20]

To raise the banner of the Lord, would make Him conspicuous to all those who gaze upon the battle. Further, it would be the very thing that the enemy would see, and with any history of battle with the Lord, would signify utter defeat to the enemy. Let's face it, Satan has lost, and will lose, every battle with God. He will never win. Each time the Lord is raised in battle, the battle is finished. Won!

Let's go to the book of John. Jesus is just a short time away from being crucified, and he is deeply troubled. In John 12, there is a powerful exchange between the Father and the Son...:

[27] "Now my soul is deeply troubled. Should I pray, 'Father, save me from this hour'? But this is the very reason I came! [28] Father, bring glory to your name." Then a voice spoke from heaven, saying, "I have already brought glory to my name, and I will do so again." [29] When the crowd heard the voice, some thought it was thunder, while others declared an angel had spoken to him. [30] Then Jesus told them, "The voice was for your benefit, not mine. [31] The time for judging this world has

---

[20] Kaiser, W. C., Jr. (1990). Exodus. In F. E. Gaebelein (Ed.), *The Expositor's Bible Commentary: Genesis, Exodus, Leviticus, Numbers* (Vol. 2, p. 409). Grand Rapids, MI: Zondervan Publishing House.

come, when Satan, the ruler of this world, will be cast out. [32] And when I am lifted up from the earth, I will draw everyone to myself." (NLT)

Think of this way. For thousands of years, the battle in the valley has raged on and on. Men have tried in vain to reach the top of the mountain to get victory but they were unable secure it. Then there were those who fought valiantly in the valley, but they too, lost severely.

It was all because the enemy in the valley was greater than any man on the mountain. But when Jesus came, He was greater than enemy man on the mountain or enemy in the valley. In fact, He came to destroy the works of the enemy.

So, He went to the cross, on a hill called Golgotha, raised His arms and stayed there for hours while the enemy taunted from the valley. What they did not know but what we do know, was that Jesus's death on that hill was not a defeat. It was not a loss. It was the very thing God used to defeat the devil once and for all, for all eternity.

The victory was won because Jesus died and when He was lifted up in the resurrection, it sealed Satan's doom.

Just like the people of Amalek, every time Moses' arms went up, they suffered loss.

The same is true for you and me. Every time we lift Jesus up above the battle we are facing and make Him our banner, we   win.

That's what Paul got. The battle rages on but that is all right, because we have victory.

[35] Can anything ever separate us from Christ's love? Does

it mean he no longer loves us if we have trouble or calamity, or are persecuted, or hungry, or destitute, or in danger, or threatened with death? [36] (As the Scriptures say, "For your sake we are killed every day; we are being slaughtered like sheep.") [37] No, despite all these things, overwhelming victory is ours through Christ, who loved us. (Romans 8:35-37, NLT)

Colossians 2 also talks about that banner…

[13] You were dead because of your sins and because your sinful nature was not yet cut away. Then God made you alive with Christ, for he forgave all our sins. [14] He canceled the record of the charges against us and took it away by nailing it to the cross. [15] In this way, he disarmed the spiritual rulers and authorities. He shamed them publicly by his victory over them on the cross. (NLT)

We don't use the cross as a trophy to show a vampire but it was on the cross that Jesus won the victory for you and me. He fought the battle, lifted up above the earth, and won it so that we could be free.

The cross, that Satan thought would bring shame to Jesus (the Bible says cursed is everyone who hangs on a tree) became my glory.

That moment Satan reveled in the death of the son of God was short-lived because that moment when Satan enjoying his victory parade was the moment it was interrupted by a Living Savior.

It's really hard to celebrate the death of the King when the King comes back from the dead.

When we lift up Jesus, it is a stinging reminder to the devil that he lost. So, lift Him up. LIFT UP JESUS!

Moses said…"They have raised their fist against the LORD's throne, so now the LORD will be at war with Amalek generation after generation." (Exodus 17:16, NLT)

God doesn't forget those that raise their fist against His Throne and He is at war with them every generation. Not just Amalek, but the very one who is at war with you. And just like a preceding generations, he wages a war that he can not win against you or God, if you will obey God, and enlist others to help you secure the victory. It is assured because Jesus already won the war.

CHAPTER 9

———➤◆◆◀———

THE PROMISE KEEPER

In the short time of God's interaction with the Jews, they had seen so many miracles. Events that were epic, defying any explanation outside of divine intervention.

Deep in the culture of the Jews was a foundation that had been established for hundreds and hundreds of years. This foundation was the powerful promises of God given to Abraham. Those promises described a people and a land that would be beyond Abraham's comprehension, but that would be shared from generation to generation in anticipation of the good things God had prepared for them.

They stood on the shoulders of Abraham, stretching to see the fulfillment of these great promises.

One evening, God told Abraham that there was coming a day that his descendants would be more innumerable than the stars in the heavens. That promise was given when there no descendants of Abraham and Sarah, and during the time in their life that they should have great-grandchildren, instead they had no child.

While the Jews could have envisioned the fulfillment of that promise, they anticipated more of a disparate host instead of a mighty nation.

The promise that was at a greater distance was the promise that Abraham's descendants would one day find a land that was beautiful and abundant beyond expectation.

So, generation after generation, they encouraged one another with the hope of these promises.

The word "promise" is a charged word, devoid of its true meaning in our culture.

Webster's Online Dictionary defines "promise" as a declaration or assurance that one will do a particular thing or that a particular thing will happen. Unfortunately, the word 'promise' means something entirely different today.

A politician promises to change the world but when they get in office, the promise to vote for legislation that align with the values of the voters is broken.

A man and woman promise to remain together, through the storms of life, but then something happens; people lose love, and that forever promise is broken.

Family members may promise a car when a teenager comes of age, but due to economic downturn that 'promise' is broken.

Sometimes promises are broken because of a circumstance, sometimes they are broken because people are evil, and sometimes the promise was not backed up with any intent to fulfill the promise.

That reminds me of the story of P.T. Barnum. One of the most incredible shows the world had seen, up until that time, was at the American Museum in New York in 1856. This museum contained a vast array of curiosities and freaks, but the most amazing highlight was the six-foot-tall "Man-Eating-Chicken."

Such a creature sounds impossible and horrific, but it was one of the key attractions of the museum. People would stand in line for hours to catch a brief glimpse of this beast. And who can blame them? After paying a few pennies for admission, they'd be ushered into a room, the curtains would be pulled back, and the stunning attraction would appear before them, just as described ...

"A tall man, seated at a table, gnawing on some chicken wings."

It was billed as "The greatest show on earth." Whatever else you say about P.T. Barnum, the mind behind the "Man Eating Chicken" attraction, the fellow knew how to woo a crowd and he was known as an entertainer. While people didn't always get exactly what they expected, they'd certainly be entertained.

Sometimes a broken promise is entertaining. Maybe like that one family member who tells you something, but every time you hear them speak, you have this "deep in the back of your mind" feeling that they cannot be trusted. But you listen anyway, knowing that you cannot fully trust what they are saying. It's a sick form of entertainment, but we have all been entertained by that family member.

Some promises feel like a bait and switch promise, where a promise is made but then in one deceptive move, the promise is 'fulfilled' with something that is less than expected, or the promise is made by someone who cannot be relied on for anything true, Satan will do everything he can to make the promises of God seem to be just one more broken or empty promise.

Broken promises are not promises at all!

Because of the hundreds of years the Jews had been in

Egypt, working as slaves, they may have felt that the promises of God were not promises at all.

Even though they had seen many miracles, God was attempting to show Himself to the people in a great demonstration of His person, not just His power and to assure them that He indeed keeps His word.

I believe this promise-making, promise-keeping God has made promises to us as well; promises that look like are never going to come to pass. We think of the moment Jesus will return to earth, and feel that it could happen at any minute, yet because it has not happened so far, we can lose faith that it will ever happen. There may be personal promises that God has made to you and until now, you have not seen the promise fulfilled.

The Jews were at Rephadim where God provided water from a rock and defeated the people of Amelek. After a period of time, God called them to the next place. In that call, God shared some of the most powerful words that any people could ever hear. In Exodus 19, "Exactly two months after the Israelites left Egypt, they arrived in the wilderness of Sinai. ² After breaking camp at Rephidim, they came to the wilderness of Sinai and set up camp there at the base of Mount Sinai. ³ Then Moses climbed the mountain to appear before God. The LORD called to him from the mountain and said, "Give these instructions to the family of Jacob; announce it to the descendants of Israel: ⁴ 'You have seen what I did to the Egyptians. You know how I carried you on eagles' wings and brought you to myself. ⁵ Now if you will obey me and keep my covenant, you will be my own special treasure from among all the peoples on earth; for all the earth belongs to me. ⁶And you will be my kingdom of priests, my holy nation.' This is the message you must give to the people of Israel." (Exodus 19:1-6, NLT)

In His own words, God declared he had carried the people of Israel on eagle's wings, soaring high above the storms, and fierce in battle.

There is a stronger word for promise that should be used in God's relationship with the Jews: Covenant. A covenant is like a promise on a two way street. God does His part and the Jews do their part. That is the strength of the covenant.

In the Old Testament, the word "covenant" was singular. The Hebrew word for covenant is "berit" meaning contract or agreement. It is a construct, which means it is grammatically bound to the maker. So, the covenant is bound to the maker of the covenant.

It is something that God wanted the Jews to know. It was not a 'promise he made' but was intrinsically bound to the personhood of God and could not be separated from Him.

It's not just important to Him that He keeps His covenant, He cannot keep from doing anything but keep His covenant. It begs the question….What is the covenant?

In the chapters that follow Exodus 19, God takes Moses up on the mountain and establishes worship requirements, the ten commandments, requirements for the sacrificial system, blueprints to build the temple, and design the ark of the covenant.

God also differentiates between clean and unclean food, the proper use of altars, fair treatment of slaves, what to do with kidnappers, and so much more.

It was all a part of the plan God had for the people, but it was a two-way street. God did His part, and the Jews did their part.

The strength of the covenant promises God made with the Jews were just as real as the ones He made with Abraham. It was a perfect covenant, one that God intended to be obeyed.

While God's covenant was perfect, it was conditional. The problem for them, and for everyone, is that God's ways are perfect, but we are not. When confronted with the conditions, the Jews could not be obedient. They failed. Sometimes they failed .1% by doing ALMOST everything God said.

For example, In 1 Samuel 15, Saul was told to go and destroy the entire Amalekite nation. He was told exactly what to do.

"Now go and completely destroy the entire Amalekite nation—men, women, children, babies, cattle, sheep, goats, camels, and donkeys." (1 Samuel 15:3, NLT)

So, Saul attacked the Amalekites, but failed to obey God completely:

"[9] Saul and his men spared Agag's life and kept the best of the sheep and goats, the cattle, the fat calves, and the lambs—everything, in fact, that appealed to them. They destroyed only what was worthless or of poor quality. [10] Then the LORD said to Samuel, [11] "I am sorry that I ever made Saul king, for he has not been loyal to me and has refused to obey my command."

Samuel was so deeply moved when he heard this that he cried out to the LORD all night." (1 Samuel 15:9-11, NLT)

Saul did 99.9 percent of what he was told to do but he found out that partial obedience is not obedience at all. Saul was actually happy he 'did what the Lord told him to do,' and told the prophet Samuel that he had carried out the Lord's command. Samuel said, 'why then am I hearing the bleating of sheep and goats?...."

In that instant, a more spiritual Saul spoke, "yes, I saved them so I could sacrifice to the Lord." But the problem was that Saul failed to follows God's command fully.

The prophet Samuel seized on the remarks with an important truth:

22 But Samuel replied, "What is more pleasing to the LORD: your burnt offerings and sacrifices or your obedience to his voice? Listen! Obedience is better than sacrifice, and submission is better than offering the fat of rams. 23 Rebellion is as sinful as witchcraft, and stubbornness as bad as worshiping idols. So because you have rejected the command of the LORD, he has rejected you as king." (Samuel 15:13-23, NLT)

God established a perfect covenant, but the problem was not the covenant or God, it was that the Jews who were imperfect.

We all are just as guilty. It is easy to come close to being obedient. It's easy to halfway be obedient, to follow most of the rules, regulations, and requirements. We can even be 99.9% obedient, almost meeting the mark.

We can be almost completely right, and at the same time

completely wrong. Sometimes it is easy for us to see other people and point out their failures, and how they miss the mark of full obedience. Compared to a pathological liar, a murderer, a rapist, we might seem to be 'better than they are,' but in reality, we miss the mark any time we are even .1% disobedient. Jesus said that if we hate someone, it can be like murder; if a man lusts after a woman, it could be the same as adultery, which puts everyone in the same category: Disobedient!

The covenant God made with the Jews was not faulty but the people were and needed a Savior.

Even today, if we tried to dot every "I," and cross every "t," then we would fail. We would fail and most would be completely freaked out by some of the requirements of the law.

For example, on the Sabbath, one could not do anything at all. They could not cook a meal, do laundry (I hear women shouting "amen" right now), or even push the button on a remote control to turn on the television (groans from the men are rising, right now).

It gets worse. The law stated that If someone broke into your house at night, and you killed that thief, according to the law, you would not be guilty of murder. If it happened in the daytime, however, you would be guilty of murder.

The Bible says that anyone who dishonors their mother or father must be put to death. Teenagers, and anyone that grew up during the 60's, 70's or 80's, are really glad that we do not follow that part of Old Testament law.

Over and over again, the law was given but along with every

requirement, every rule, every regulation, an all encompassing truth would emerge: the people would not and could not fulfill it.

God knew all of this, even before He gave the requirements. We know He knew that the Jews would be unable to fully obey because at the same time He gave them the requirements, He provided a series of sacrifices that would push back their transgression.

On the day of atonement, Aaron would sacrifice an animal and present the blood of that animal before God. It would be repeated every year, because it only covered up sin, it would not take it away. On that day, the high priest would sacrifice a bull for a sin offering, a ram for a burnt offering, and a goat for a sin offering.

He would confess the nation's sin and then present it before God. When the day of atonement occurred on the fiftieth year, it was called the year of jubilee, a day that slaves were set free, property was restored to families, and debt was forgiven.

Sin sacrifices happened once a year, and people were set free every fifty years. As you can see, the covenant God set up was designed to point out that we were not perfect, built around sacrifices that we not perfect either. Sin sacrifices once a year and setting people free every fifty years is not ideal or adequate.

What the Jews did not know was that old covenant was only a template God would use to point people to something better. They needed something better with a covenant designed to set free the sinner every single day. They needed a better covenant and a better sacrifice.

So do we.

So, an Amazing God planned long before man was created to do just that: provide a better sacrifice built on a stronger covenant. One sealed with the blood of His own son:

Hebrews 8 says: "⁶But now Jesus, our High Priest, has been given a ministry that is far superior to the old priesthood, for he is the one who mediates for us a far better covenant with God, based on better promises. ⁷If the first covenant had been faultless, there would have been no need for a second covenant to replace it. ⁸But when God found fault with the people, he said: "The day is coming, says the LORD, when I will make a new covenant with the people of Israel and Judah. ⁹This covenant will not be like the one I made with their ancestors when I took them by the hand and led them out of the land of Egypt. They did not remain faithful to my covenant, so I turned my back on them, says the LORD. ¹⁰But this is the new covenant I will make with the people of Israel on that day, says the LORD: I will put my laws in their minds, and I will write them on their hearts. I will be their God, and they will be my people. (Hebrews 8:6-10, NLT)

God knew the old covenant was not enough and used the old covenant to do two things: First, point out our faults and failures, to show us our disobedience, and second, to show us a redeemer, a savior that could set us free.

The Apostle Paul, in his great understanding of the covenant and old testament law wrote the Galatians (Chapter 3:19-22): ¹⁹Why, then, was the law given? It was given alongside the promise to show people their sins. But the law was designed to last only until the coming of the child who was promised. God gave his law through angels to Moses, who was the mediator between God and the people. [20] Now a mediator is helpful if more than one party must reach an agreement. But God, who is one, did not use a mediator when he gave his promise to Abraham.

[21] Is there a conflict, then, between God's law and God's promises? Absolutely not! If the law could give us new life, we could be made right with God by obeying it. [22] But the Scriptures declare that we are all prisoners of sin, so we receive God's promise of freedom only by believing in Jesus Christ. (NLT)

We receive God's promise of freedom only by believing in Jesus Christ. There is no other way and the law was inadequate to do that, by design. By showing how impossible it is to keep the law, but also understanding the necessity of obedience, God used something greater than the law to change us, He used the power of His Holy Spirit and the changing power of the cross to bring us to a place of redemption and salvation. Look closely at verse 10:

[10] But those who depend on the law to make them right with God are under his curse, for the Scriptures say, "Cursed is everyone who does not observe and obey all the commands that are written in God's Book of the Law." [11] So it is clear that no one can be made right with God by trying to keep the law. For the Scriptures say, "It is through faith that a righteous person has life." [12] This way of faith is very different from the way of

law, which says, "It is through obeying the law that a person has life."

¹³ But Christ has rescued us from the curse pronounced by the law. When he was hung on the cross, he took upon himself the curse for our wrongdoing. For it is written in the Scriptures, "Cursed is everyone who is hung on a tree." (Galatians 3:10-13, NLT)

The old covenant had run its course and pointed people to the cross.

The writer to the Hebrews noted, ¹¹ So Christ has now become the High Priest over all the good things that have come. He has entered that greater, more perfect Tabernacle in heaven, which was not made by human hands and is not part of this created world. ¹² With his own blood—not the blood of goats and calves—he entered the Most Holy Place once for all time and secured our redemption forever.

¹³ Under the old system, the blood of goats and bulls and the ashes of a heifer could cleanse people's bodies from ceremonial impurity. ¹⁴ Just think how much more the blood of Christ will purify our consciences from sinful deeds so that we can worship the living God. For by the power of the eternal Spirit, Christ offered himself to God as a perfect sacrifice for our sins. ¹⁵ That is why he is the one who mediates a new covenant between God and people, so that all who are called can receive the eternal inheritance God has promised them. For Christ died to set them free from the penalty of the sins they had committed under that first covenant. (Hebrews 9:11-15, NLT)

I find this amazing: God gave rules, regulations, laws, and a covenant with the full knowledge that we needed more than rules. He gave them because He knew we did not know what we needed. We needed a savior. We were hopeless, helpless, *and clueless.*

He gave the Old Testament covenant with the full knowledge that we couldn't keep it, so He built in it the sacrifices that would help the people understand that they needed a Savior.

But it was not enough. The sacrifices were not powerful enough, the blood was not strong enough, the covenant was not life changing enough. It did serve to push back the sin, but did not change the sinner. The law did not have the power to change a person's heart, nor the power to keep a rule.

It's the same in civil society. There are millions of laws on the books, and still, there are people who break the law, go to jail or prison, and when they are released, do the same crime and the cycle continues. It brings to bear the truth that the law cannot change us.

So in the mind of our Amazing God, He had a plan to send us someone who could do all we needed done, one that would be a sacrifice that was greater than any other, one who would give us power to obey, not because a requirement, but because of love for God, and one who would make it possible for us to know God with more than a head knowledge or through a sacrifice of a goat, a bull, or any other animal.

God would take His law and write it on our hearts through the death of His very own son. God would take our sin, and place our sin on His perfect sacrifice: HIS SON and cleanse our sin.

Isaiah saw it coming when he wrote, "³ He was despised and rejected— a man of sorrows, acquainted with deepest grief. We turned our backs on him and looked the other way. He was despised, and we did not care.

⁴ Yet it was our weaknesses he carried; it was our sorrows that weighed him down. And we thought his troubles were a punishment from God, a punishment for his own sins! ⁵ But he was pierced for our rebellion, crushed for our sins. He was beaten so we could be whole. He was whipped so we could be healed. ⁶ All of us, like sheep, have strayed away. We have left God's paths to follow our own. Yet the LORD laid on him the sins of us all. (Isaiah 53:3-6, NLT)

Even today, there are those who feel the brunt of guilt and shame. Even though they have never read the rules or regulations, there is a deep sense of wrongness. They know there is something missing, something wrong, something needed.

They feel lonely and they feel lost but God in His Amazing way, has provided a way for anyone who feels guilt, shame, lost, and lonely to experience the joy and peace of knowing Jesus Christ. God provided a more than sufficient savior through Christ; one who can forgive, wash away the transgression and cleanse us from our past deeds.

The words God spoke to the Jews in earlier verses declare the heart of God for you today:

You know how I carried you on eagles' wings and brought

you to myself. ⁵ Now if you will obey me and keep my covenant, you will be my own special treasure from among all the peoples on earth; for all the earth belongs to me. ⁶ And you will be my kingdom of priests, my holy nation.'

There is a fantastic passage in 1 Peter that sounds almost identical to this passage. For anyone who accepts Jesus Christ as their Savior, they enjoy the same love from the Father as the Jews did:

⁹ But you are not like that, for you are a chosen people. You are royal priests, a holy nation, God's very own possession. As a result, you can show others the goodness of God, for he called you out of the darkness into his wonderful light. ¹⁰ "Once you had no identity as a people; now you are God's people. Once you received no mercy; now you have received God's mercy." (1 Peter 2:9-10, NLT)

The heart of our Amazing God is for everyone to experience the reality of this verse. To know about God is great, but to know God is amazing!

CHAPTER 10

------- ◆ -------

IT IS PERSONAL

Sometimes it is easy to see how God could speak to certain people. They are the heroes, the wealthy, the coolest people on the planet. They were the one's that anyone would want to speak to, including the God of the universe. Included in this "God speaks to…" hall of fame would be Abraham, David, Moses, Noah and a few other men who somehow had what we do not:

God spoke to them because they were what we are not: perfect.

For those unsure that God would want to speak them about anything, they would wonder what would God say. And if He did talk to them, who would He sound like? Would the voice of God sound like your mom: "Now Johnny…you know what you need to do…" Would His voice sound like your dad? "Don't make me pull this car to the side of the side of the road…." We heard that a lot on vacations. Dad never pulled the car over, but the threat gave him a measly thirty seconds of peace.

For some, they think the voice of God would sound like the voice of the one who hands out discipline: mean, exacting, and filled with the desire inflict the worst kind of punishment.

For some, they never think of God speaking, nor doing

anything personal, or even noticing them.   Therapy moment here: Growing up as a middle child, I always felt like I was never noticed. I felt like a ghost. A non-person. In school, I wasn't noticed unless I did something wrong.   The cool quarterback for our high school was noticed all the time. Even if I were to wave my arms, scream as loud as I could to get someone to notice me, there would be someone who would say, "stop waiving your hands, sit down and shut up, we are waiting for someone that matters to come along." Once I even planned my own surprise birthday party. I was only six years old, but felt that I was not going to have a celebration, so I invited my friends to my surprise birthday party. I'll never forget the 'surprise' on mom's face when kids and parents showed up for my surprise party. It was a surprise, only for mom. And the scolding I received after that 'surprise' party is the reason my right eye twitches today.

Sometimes that feeling of being a ghost translates into the way we think that God feels about us. We have the overwhelming feeling that we don't matter, or that God is a lot more interested in someone else, and that we are only a bother. If we were to wave our arms to God, screaming out for Him to pay attention to us, that the best we could hope for is for God to say, "Shut up, I am waiting for someone like Abraham to call on me."

On your best day, you may feel that God is ignoring you, or that He, the God of all creation, would say to you, "LEAVE ME ALONE!"

I wonder if the individual Jew felt this way as they migrated from Egypt to the promised land. I wonder if the individual Jew ever wondered if God could be personal, caring, and interested in them. I wonder if they every thought of God as a friend.

I am sure it was a foreign thought to their mind. God was a friend to Moses. He cared a lot about Lot, and was interested in what Abraham thought about things, but to consider God desiring to have an intimate relationship with an individual outside the chosen few was unheard of, and probably forbidden to consider.

It is very clear however, that as God was revealing Himself to a nation, He was doing so in a stepped fashion. His desire was to lead the people past 'group think' and into a personal walk with Him. "Group think" is a term that is a kissing-cousin to peer pressure, except it is for adults only, who let the crowd determine their response.

It was going to get extremely personal, by God's design, and that He would use all of the struggles to bring the people to a place where they would see Him in a personal way. It was about to get really personal.

After God gave the people instructions on worship, the law, and life at Mt. Sinai, he eventually led them to the place they had only dreamed about. In fact, at this point, they were poised to go into the promised land just a few hundred feet away.

Up until now, God had done amazing things for the Jews. There were times they saw the mighty hand of God and there was NO DOUBT God had performed miracles that could not be explained by natural phenomenon.

Eventually, God brings us all to a place where a crisis moment confronts us. It could be a place where the decision may be life or death, peace or drama, joy or pain. But rarely are we confronted with THE decision of a lifetime. If the right decision is made, then blessing and life comes, but if not, then death is clearly the alternative.

As the Jews were standing at the edge of the promised land, no decision had been more crucial and life-impacting than this one. It was epic!

For hundreds of years, the Jews told their kids, and their kids told their children's kids that there was coming a day when they would make it to the Promised Land. Now, for millions of Jews, that long-promised plan was unfolding. They were THE generation when the promise would be fulfilled if they obeyed.

Now, the one thing that God wanted them to understand was that every struggle, crisis, and desperate moment they faced were primers to help them see an Amazing God who could do anything. It should have been a culmination of experience that would drive them to make the right choices, to believe God for every need, and to trust the heart of God for every situation.

In the most powerful way, this moment did not arrive out of nowhere. But make no mistake about it at all: this was THE MOMENT. If they missed it; they would miss it completely. There would be no do-overs. No second chances. No plan "B." This was it.

God instructs Moses to send twelve men into the Promised

Land, essentially to bring back a report about the inhabitants, the crops, the challenges and opportunities that they found. The men were chosen from each tribe of the Jews. Each tribe was a descendant of one of Jacob's twelve sons. They were family and they had all experienced the same Amazing God and His work in their lives.

The instructions were clear:[17] Moses gave the men these instructions as he sent them out to explore the land: "Go north through the Negev into the hill country. [18] See what the land is like, and find out whether the people living there are strong or weak, few or many. [19] See what kind of land they live in. Is it good or bad? Do their towns have walls, or are they unprotected like open camps? [20] Is the soil fertile or poor? Are there many trees? Do your best to bring back samples of the crops you see." (It happened to be the season for harvesting the first ripe grapes.) (Numbers 12:17-19, NLT)

So these twelve men were sent to explore the land. They saw everything; the land, the people, the challenges, everything:

[23] When they came to the valley of Eshcol, they cut down a branch with a single cluster of grapes so large that it took two of them to carry it on a pole between them! They also brought back samples of the pomegranates and figs. (Numbers 12:23, NLT)

As they journeyed through the land for forty days, they experienced the reality of God's promises. After the forty days, they returned to the Jews and Moses to report their findings.

[27] This was their report to Moses: "We entered the land you

sent us to explore, and it is indeed a bountiful country—a land flowing with milk and honey. Here is the kind of fruit it produces. [28] But the people living there are powerful, and their towns are large and fortified. We even saw giants there, the descendants of Anak! [29] The Amalekites live in the Negev, and the Hittites, Jebusites, and Amorites live in the hill country. The Canaanites live along the coast of the Mediterranean Sea and along the Jordan Valley." [30] But Caleb tried to quiet the people as they stood before Moses. "Let's go at once to take the land," he said. "We can certainly conquer it!" [31] But the other men who had explored the land with him disagreed. "We can't go up against them! They are stronger than we are!" [32] So they spread this bad report about the land among the Israelites: "The land we traveled through and explored will devour anyone who goes to live there. All the people we saw were huge. [33] We even saw giants there, the descendants of Anak. Next to them we felt like grasshoppers, and that's what they thought, too!" (Numbers 13:25-33, NLT)

This created great fear with the people: "Then the whole community began weeping aloud, and they cried all night. [2] Their voices rose in a great chorus of protest against Moses and Aaron. "If only we had died in Egypt, or even here in the wilderness!" they complained. [3] "Why is the LORD taking us to this country only to have us die in battle? Our wives and our little ones will be carried off as plunder! Wouldn't it be better for us to return to Egypt?" [4] Then they plotted among themselves, "Let's choose a new leader and go back to Egypt!" (Numbers 14:1-4, NLT)

For two years since leaving Egypt, the people had seen just how Amazing God really was, as He destroyed the Egyptians in the Red Sea and helped them defeat the people of Amalek. Now they felt that these enemies were greater and more powerful than their abilities and their God. They felt trapped and severely overwhelmed by the situation.

Think about this for a minute. It was God who told them to go and spy out the land. If God brought them to it, told them to go into it, and promised that they would inherit the land, then it stands to reason that the only thing that could hold them back from their destiny is what they did with the information and weigh it against the history they had with God.

It's not too often where one decision determines a destiny, but there are a few.

When I decided to marry my wife, that decision determined my destiny. The marriage has produced three incredible children and a very blessed man in me. That decision determined my destiny.

The night I attended Oak Hill Church to hear a former member of a Hell's Angels Motorcycle Gang member share his testimony of salvation determined my destiny. In fact, as I sat in the service listening as this "bad to the bone" former gang member share his story, I thought to myself: "I have never thought about *any* of the things he attempted." I didn't even own a motorcycle, although at one time I did rock a seriously yellow moped (don't judge me). I could not identify with the man's struggles or exploits, but the one thing I did identify with was sin. He shared that the same God that would send a Hell's Angels Motorcycle gang member to hell because of sin, would send anyone who had sin in their life. I was guilty of being a sinner, and felt the conviction of the Holy Spirit. In fact, it felt as if every eye in the church was on me, telling me I was a sinner. No one was looking at me, but conviction sometimes can feel like everyone sees everything. As he finished his talk, he invited everyone who had sin in their lives to come and accept the generous gift of salvation that God had offered to everyone, and anyone who would accept it.

To think that a God who finds sin so offensive to His holiness would choose to provide a remedy to that offense, so He could spend eternity with us amazed me, and still does.

That moment, when I knelt in submission to Christ, asked Him to forgive me and wash me determined my eternal destiny. At that moment, I became a Christ follower and have not regretted one minute of that journey.

When we said yes to God to start a church in Elkhart, Indiana, it turned into a destiny God is still writing.

My personal decision to follow Christ, to answer the call to ministry, those have all been destiny decisions. But, each decision was a significant personal decision. It was not decided by committee or even spiritual advisors. Ultimately, it was a personal decision that God presented to me, and that I accepted, or agreed to follow.

The Jews, tied up in group thinking, were facing a moment so life-changing and epic that no other decision could compare. The decision would literally mean the difference between life in a beautiful land, flowing with the best produce and cattle grazing on the hills and well fed sheep, or spending the rest of their life in the desert, trying to live out an existence on meager fare.

Most did not choose wisely, except there were saner heads that tried to speak life into the situation:

⁶ Two of the men who had explored the land, Joshua son of Nun and Caleb son of Jephunneh, tore their clothing. ⁷ They said to all the people of Israel, "The land we traveled through and explored is a wonderful land! ⁸ And if the LORD is pleased with us, he will bring us safely into that land and give it to us. It is a rich land flowing with milk and honey. ⁹ Do not rebel against the LORD, and don't be afraid of the people of the land. They are only helpless prey to us! They have no protection, but the LORD is with us! Don't be afraid of them!" (Numbers 14:6-9, NLT)

I believe there is an underlying thought behind Joshua and Caleb's call to the people. It's not clearly defined, but I believe they were trying to say something…that is not readily apparent in these verses…and that is this fact: this is personal!

If the Lord is pleased with us…He will bring us safely into that land and give it to us…It is a rich land flowing with milk and honey…prepared for us…make a personal decision right now…because God has been with us and has led us to this moment!

THIS IS PERSONAL…Do not rebel against the Lord.

THIS IS PERSONAL…Don't be afraid of the people of the land.

They are only helpless prey to us! THIS IS PERSONAL!!!
They have no protection…THIS IS PERSONAL!!!!
The Lord is with us….THIS IS PERSONAL.
Don't be afraid of them.

Joshua and Caleb had a courage inside of them that rose up when they considered the decision in front of them. They saw the same things as the other spies. They were not like Pollyanna that thinks the sky is blue and butterflies always fill the meadow…that if one pretends something is ok…pleasant thoughts will make it ok.

That kind of thinking drives me crazy. I really struggle when the situation is really bad, and someone pretends that it is not that bad. And they believe by pretending it is not as bad, then believing that it is not as bad, will make it not as bad. My mind spins with frustration. I believe we should be honest about the situation.

For example, if a doctor says that tests have indicated cancer and that the cancer has progressed to the point of no return, I believe it is imperative to be honest about what the tests concluded. Being honest does not tie God's hands or impede His ability to do amazing things, it just helps form the basis for the awesome miracle He can perform.

Do you know what else drives me crazy? When someone sees how bad it is, they refuse to believe God can do something about it. They think that fate has dealt them a blow and they should just accept and deal with it, without taking it to God in prayer. I have experienced too many blessings, witnessed too many miracles to think that God has become powerless.

Both types of thinking are harmful: those which pretend every thing is all right and assume this thinking will make it all right, when it's not, and those who see how bad it is and forget that God can do amazing things!

Joshua and Caleb did not ignore what they saw, they just compared the challenge to their experience with God. They were honest and every time they compared their giants to God, they were more convinced that God is bigger and that His promises are more believable than what they experienced in the Promised Land.

Everyone has that moment when confronted with the reality of a moment. It usually is bigger than we can handle, but for anyone who has any experience with God, they should compare the problem with the all-surpassing awesomeness of God. There really is no comparison. The same God who spoke creation into existence is the same one who can defeat any enemy, perform any work He desires, and can overcome any obstacle.

This is where someone will share an oft-repeated cliché: "Remember, God will never put more on you than you can handle." This is a variant of a passage that discusses temptation, not trials. Unfortunately, most people believe the 'out of context' part, and refuse to believe the "take the next exit" promise that God has for those who face temptation. When it comes to trials, or in Joshua and Caleb's case, GIANTS, it was certain

God DID put more on them than they could handle

Simply because GOD WANTED TO HANDLE IT for them, just like He wants to do for you!

They knew God was bigger, stronger, mightier, and greater than anything or anyone they could face. They took that personally.

If you have very little experience with God, it may be difficult to compare your experience with God next to your problem. In those cases, it is important to read the stories of others who faced giants, walled cities, massive armies, drought and famine, and see how their problems compared to their God. In circumstance after circumstance, God proved greater than they could ever hope for. The beauty of these stories is that the same God that did them desires for you to know Him the same way they knew God.

As you read these incredible stories, begin to trust God to do the same for you. Read them and know that He is able to do even more, and that His love for you is great, and His power has not diminished over time.

But, it is important to get this one thing. All of the problems you will face are not to destroy you, but to help you understand and know an Amazing God who will use whatever we go through to reveal Himself to us in greater measure.

And it will be personal.

Your family may be affected by the circumstances, but it will be extremely personal for every member of the family. The choices that are made at that point will change everything, even if only one makes the right choice. A destiny is at stake and the choices that are made determine the outcome of that destiny.

Caleb and Joshua stood up and implored the people to believe that God would bring them safely into the Promised Land. But the people began talking about stoning Joshua and Caleb. That moment of destiny had taken a turn for the very worst. After all God had done for the people and revealed himself in ways that no nation had ever experienced was now a moment of great disappointment for God. At the moment the people were openly talking about stoning the men of faith, the people who believed God could do anything, the Bible says that the glorious presence of the Lord appeared to all the Israelites at the Tabernacle.

When the Bible declared that the 'glorious presence of the Lord appeared,' it might seem like a good thing, but think about that one time when you have had enough with your kids and warning after warning went unheeded, and then you will have a sense of why this event was not good for the people. They not only missed their one and only opportunity to go into the Promised Land they also made God so angry that He was ready to destroy the Jews.

They knew better. The choice was theirs, and now the moment for the people to enter the Promised Land was gone.

There would not be another. God would send them into the desert again, and He let them know that because they failed to believe God, they would be destroyed if they tried to enter in to the land without God.

They were sent into the desert for forty years. Each one would die there except for the two that believed and trusted an Amazing God: Joshua and Caleb. Everyone else would die without ever putting one foot into the Promised Land. They failed their one and only chance to go into the promised land.

It's not always that we have one decision that impacts us so much, that by choosing, the decision so affects destiny.

I am reminded that a long time before the world began, God made a decision to send his son to the world. That one decision potentially affected mankind's destiny. Jesus had a decision too. When he was on the earth, He knew exactly that He would one day die for the sins of the world. There was a decision moment for Him too. It was the night before He was put on a cross.

He was praying in a place called the Garden of Gethsemane. While He was there, the Bible says that Jesus was in such agony, as He was deciding whether he would give His life for you and me, that scripture says His sweat became drops of blood.

It's almost like He was at the edge of the Promised Land and He knew what it meant to go over.

If He gave his life for men and women, then the world could be saved. Men and women, boys and girls could become sons and daughters of God. People could be set free from the things that held them back, the things that kept them bound, and He knew the power of the moment but it has to be said that Jesus had a choice. He could have said, "Father, these people are not worth me giving my life." He had a choice. Thank God, he could have said that…but instead He said:

Father, if you are willing, please take this cup of suffering away from me. Yet I want your will to be done, not mine." (Luke 22:42, NLT)

He knew exactly what that cup of suffering would mean. It don't know what the cup of suffering would feel like. In my mind, I think that pain from nails driven through His hands and feet would be a 'cup of suffering.' That certainly would hurt.

I might think that a 'cup of suffering' could be thorns made into a crown and pressed into His skull. That would be extremely painful.

I would possibly think of a 'cup of suffering' would be being beat with a whip that had shards of iron and glass embedded in the ends of it, ripping the skin on the one being whipped. That would be excruciating.

I believe the suffering was not just the physical. It was the fact that my sin, and your sin, in one moment, was placed on Jesus. The only one never having experienced sin was now having the sin of the world placed on Him. In that moment, a completely innocent man was condemned to death. Not just death in the physical sense, but for a moment, the one who had never been separated from His Father was now about to be separated from God for a moment while He took on himself the sins of every man and woman, every girl and boy.

He had a choice and His decisions determined my destiny!

Jesus chose to suffer so that we could be free. He gave His life so we could have a personal relationship with God. He suffered so powerfully, so that I could never be separated from God.

He made it personal, so I could know the Father.

I don't know who the worst person on the planet is at this very moment. I can't imagine who would win the 'most evil' award, if there were such a thing. Whoever that is, along with everyone else, are the very ones that Jesus came and died for, the one that he offers forgiveness to today.

It may be a Hell's Angel Motorcycle gang member, or a seriously bad to the bone yellow moped riding dude like me, these are the people Jesus came and died for, because we all needed a Savior.

That amazes me.

The very fact that Jesus would decide to leave heaven, become a man, live a sinless life and then, in one fateful decision, decide to die for me overwhelms me.

That He would, for a moment of time, feel the pain of separation from God because of my sin is incomprehensible.

And then, after enduring the cross, and suffering my shame, would offer to forgive me, cleanse me, and make me a child of God in out of anything I could ever deserve or hope for.

Yet that is just what Jesus did for me. He died for me and made it personal.

That is why the offer of salvation is so epic. Without this salvation, a person who dies will spend eternity in hell. Far worse than missing the Promised Land, for the Jews still had the presence of God with them until they died. The decision to dismiss this offer of salvation will leave the man or woman with an eternity of pain and suffering, but worse than that, will leave them without the presence of God. That is the worst part of hell!

The decisions that the Jews made led them to the desert, to die there. They were never allowed in, except Joshua and Caleb, and most of their remaining forty years they would be about a two week journey from the Promised Land.

There are a lot of decisions we make that change us for a minute. Some change us for a few months, but the decision whether to accept Christ as Savior and Lord is the one decision that will literally affect us forever.

It's like we are all standing on the banks of the river Jordan, and with one decision, are allowed to experience a life with God that is amazing, or if we refuse, spend the rest of our day without joy, peace and abundant life, and then, in the end, find the rejection of salvation destined us to a forever that never ends, one filled with hopelessness, darkness, and alienated from the presence of God forever.

This is going to sound like a preacher, but don't miss the power of what an Amazing God He really is...for in God's heart, He knows that a sinner cannot stay in His presence. It is impossible. He could have destroyed the earth when Adam and Eve sinned...and could send lightning strikes to sinners at the moment they commit their sin, just so that 'sinners are dealt with...' but instead, He chose to send the remedy. Why in the world would anyone do such a thing? Jesus said it was because of love:

[16] "For this is how God loved the world: He gave his one and only Son, so that everyone who believes in him will not perish but have eternal life. [17] God sent his Son into the world not to judge the world, but to save the world through him. (John 3:16-17, NLT)

Scripture further declares that God is not willing that anyone die without Christ, but is patient so that people will repent.

There are hundreds of scripture references that declare God's love and desire for us to know Him, and He is constantly seeking out men and women to have some kind of experience that will open their hearts door to at least have a moment to consider beginning a walk to follow Christ.

Even in the wandering in the desert, God always wanted the Jews to experience all that He promised, and more importantly, He wanted them to experience WHO HE IS...and in that, have a personal relationship with God.

Now, this gets personal. God wants the same thing for you. In every part of your life, God has quietly been waiting for you to turn and look His direction. He has allowed some things to happen, some good and some bad, not to hurt you, but to bring you to a place where you would say, "God, I need you," or "God, where are you?" or "God, why me?" Those times were not to destroy you, but to bring you to a red sea experience, a dry place in the desert, a place of hunger, or maybe just a place where it seems that every frog, locust, and gnat in a twenty mile radius had found your home, all for the purpose of introducing you to the only one who truly loves you. The only one who really does have your eternal best interest at heart, and has a plan for your life that is AMAZING…one that correlates with who God is.

He wants you to know Him as God, and as friend. He wants you to experience Him as the water you thirst for, and the bread you seek after. He wants to be the one who fights your battles, who gives you instructions on how to live and how to love. He wants to be YOUR GOD. He wants you to be HIS PEOPLE. He wants to show you great and mighty things that you could never experience in this life without Him.

He wants to calm your storm, walk on the water, and get in your boat. He wants to take a few fish and loaves of bread and mass produce enough to meet your needs to the full. He wants to speak to you, share stories with you, and show you love in a way that no one has ever experienced.

It is personal! He wants you to know Him in a greater way than anyone else, and more than ever before. He desires a close intimate relationship with you that brings you to Him, just as you are!

In my daily reading, I came across the rules God was giving the people of Israel as they wandered in the wilderness. In those regulations, God specifically said, "if a woman has an issue of blood, she is unclean." In that regulation was the answer to her purification, and she had to do certain things in order to be clean. After a period of time, she could be considered clean again. What struck me about that passage was that anyone who came in contact with her, in certain situations would be unclean if they touched her. It sounded cruel to ostracize her from the people because of something beyond her control. I understand that God sometimes does that to show something bigger, and the very same day that Old Testament reading was on my list, the New Testament reading was the story of the woman who sought Jesus out because she had suffered with an issue of blood for twelve years, never finding relief. In the law, she was unclean and not supposed to touch anything holy.

That was until Jesus came along. She heard that He was in the area and sought him out. She found the crowd surrounding Him and pressed in with all she had just to touch the hem of His garment. Even though she was unclean, and He was holy, she knew that He was her only hope.

Of course, when she touched the hem of Jesus' robe, she was instantly healed and He knew someone had touched Him. For me the amazing part of this exchange was His response to the woman. When He questioned who touched His robe, the woman confessed that she was the one and why she touched Him. He looked at her and said, "Daughter, your faith has made you well. Go in peace. Your suffering is over." (Mark 5:34, NLT)

The law was not meant to push people away from God, but to help them understand in a greater way, their very need FOR GOD. In this setting, the woman was made whole because she found out that God wants us 'just the way we are,' and that by touching Him, we are set free from everything that keeps us from being clean.

It is very personal, and God wants you and me, just the way we are. Whether you are a bad boy to the bone, yellow moped rocking dude like me, or a milder "Harley" rider, God loves you and desires for you to know an AMAZING GOD.

I did, and every day, He is more amazing to me than the day before.

FINAL WORDS

———◆◆———

FROM JOHN UTLEY

If you have never surrendered your life to Jesus Christ, today is your day. God spent years attempting to reveal Himself to several million Jews and most did not understand what He was wanting to do for them and in them. All of that found it's realization in Jesus Christ. He was the remedy to every problem man has, and because of His sacrifice on the cross, we can have redemption through His blood. Today, if you do not know Him, take this moment and accept Jesus Christ as your Lord and Savior.

God Loves You!
God loves you so much that he made a way for you, through the shed blood of his son so that you might be able to spend eternity with Him.

"For God so loved the world that he gave His only Begotten Son, that whosoever believeth in Him should not perish, but have Everlasting Life" (Jn. 3:16).

Man is a Sinner, and Sin has Separated him from God!

You may think you are a good person but being good is not enough! Every man has sinned and there is none that is righteous before God!

"For all have sinned and come short of the Glory of God" (Rom. 3:23).

Jesus Christ is the Only Remedy for Sin!

Jesus Christ is the only remedy for sin. We can not be good enough to get into heaven, nor can our good works get us there.

There was no other way for God to erase the effect of sin except by blood. The shedding of Christ's blood indicated that the penalty for sin had been paid; a perfect sinless life had been sacrificed for the lives of all who have sinned.

". . .Without the shedding of blood, there is no forgiveness of sins" (Hebrews 9:22)
"For Christ also hath once suffered for sins, the just for the unjust, that He might bring us to God..." (I Pet. 3:18).
"Neither is there Salvation in any other: for there is none other name under Heaven given among men, whereby we must be saved" (Acts 4:12).
You Must Receive Jesus Christ as Your Lord and Savior
To be saved, a man must confess that Jesus is Lord, while acknowledging in his heart that Christ must have full rule over his life. This confession of Christ as Lord assumes that it is Christ who will work and fulfill His own righteousness within man, as man is unable to attain righteousness of his own accord.

Jesus calls this experience the "new birth." He told Nicodemus: ". . . Except a man be born again, he cannot see the Kingdom of God" (Jn. 3:3).
We invite you now to receive the Lord Jesus Christ as your personal Saviour. "But as many as received Him, to them gave He power to become the sons of God, even to them that believe

on His Name" (Jn. 1:12).

Pray this Prayer and Mean it with all Your Heart

Dear Lord Jesus, I realize that I am a sinner and have broken your laws. I understand that my sin has separated me from you. I am sorry and I ask you to forgive me. I accept the fact that your son Jesus Christ died for me, was resurrected, and is alive today and hears my prayers. I now open my heart's door and invite Jesus in to become my Lord and my Saviour. I give Him control and ask that He would rule and reign in my heart so that His perfect will would be accomplished in my life. In Jesus name I pray. Amen.
Congratulations!

If you prayed this prayer in all sincerity, you are now a Child of God. However there are a few things that you need to do to follow up on your commitment.

- Get baptized (full immersion) in water as commanded by Christ
- Tell someone else about your new faith in Christ.
- Spend time with God each day through prayer and Bible reading
- Seek fellowship with other followers of Jesus at a Bible believing church

Write the author at John Utley, P.O. Box 840, Granger, IN 46530

ABOUT

———◆◆———

JOHN UTLEY

John Utley serves as Lead Pastor of Radiant Life Church in Elkhart, Indiana. He lived in Arkansas for most of his life, until God called his family to Northern Indiana. Their ministry has taken them to Israel, Mexico, Ecuador, Japan, Chile, Venzuela, and Honduras. They have ministered in person or via the Internet (Radiant Word) to people in over 35 states and every continent. John earned his Bachelor of Science degree in Church Ministries from Southwestern Assemblies of God University in Waxahachie, Texas. He has served churches in Arkansas and Indiana. John loves writing, and published his first book, "When God Says Nothing" in 2010. He has written several articles printed in national and regional publications; he has ministered on radio and television. John is married to Susan (Craig) and they recently celebrated their 30th Wedding anniversary. They have been in ministry together since 1985. John serves on the board of the Northern Indiana Teen Challenge Center. He has led seventeen overseas short term missions teams.

A companion guide for small group use will be available late fall 2016. For more information, check out the author's blog: www.johnutley.com